SERVANT OF ALL

Servant of All

*Status, Ambition,
and the Way of Jesus*

CRAIG C. HILL

WILLIAM B. EERDMANS PUBLISHING COMPANY
GRAND RAPIDS, MICHIGAN

Wm. B. Eerdmans Publishing Co.
2140 Oak Industrial Drive N.E., Grand Rapids, Michigan 49505
www.eerdmans.com

© 2016 Craig C. Hill
Published 2016
Printed in the United States of America

22 21 20 19 18 17 16   1 2 3 4 5 6 7

ISBN 978-0-8028-7362-0

Library of Congress Cataloging-in-Publication Data

A catalog record for this book is available from the Library of Congress

Jesus sat down, called the twelve, and said to them,
"Whoever wants to be first must be last of all and servant of all."

MARK 9:35

CONTENTS

FOREWORD

Hello. I am a member of Phi Beta Kappa, have earned degrees from three different colleges and universities, picked up honorary degrees from a dozen more, and have written seventy books. Did I mention that I am a bishop and a member of the faculty at a university? I also have better-than-average cholesterol numbers and have never committed adultery.

Glad to meet you. My name is Will. What is your name, and how can I use you to position me even higher up the pecking order?

I can think of few people better qualified than I to write a foreword to Craig Hill's fast-paced, revealing, scholarly-without-being-showy, and pointedly practical book on status and ambition. I wish I had *Servant of All: Status, Ambition, and the Way of Jesus* when I was a young pastor attempting to lead my first rural Methodist congregation. The preening and jockeying for position that occurred among members of my flock were a discredit to their Christian faith. If I had this book then, I would have understood them better. Later, I could have used this book when I joined the faculty at a divinity school. I could have utilized the insights on ambition to wallop some of those pompous, posturing, and pretentious senior faculty divines.

Having served some years as a professor, I know why, after many years of teaching at Oxford and Cambridge, C. S. Lewis defined Hell as, "where everyone is perpetually concerned about his own dignity and advancement, where everyone has a grievance, and where everyone lives the deadly serious passions of envy, self-importance, and resentment" (Preface to the 1961 edition of *The Screwtape Letters*).

Not content to expose the ambitiousness and status-seeking of others, *Servant of All* ruthlessly exposes mine. With time, I grew up, learned how to clamber up the ladder, and showed that I could play status-seek with the pushiest of them. I got ordained, got tenure, got published, and got elected bishop without appearing to be desperately campaigning for election. (Few joys are greater than to have folks bestow high status upon you without knowing that thereby they are fueling the worst aspects of your personality.)

But hey, why beat up on myself for my get-up-and-go? Craig Hill shows that ambition, desire for superior status, assessment of ourselves by comparison with others, is a perfectly natural, innate, widespread, and all-too-human tendency. Ambition—our desire to be and to create something better than others—leads to some of our most noble achievements.

Craig charitably recognizes that pastors (and surely he would include bishops) are in a tough position in regard to the vice of ambition: "It takes a certain amount of ambition to jump through the many hoops required to enter ordained ministry. . . . It takes an even higher level of ambition to tackle with energy, eagerness, and imagination a long-term appointment at a church. I cannot imagine a fruitful pastor who is not ambitious, who does not dream dreams, see visions, and then work vigorously toward their realization."

Status, honor, and the drive to get ahead would be worthy human endeavor *if it were not for Jesus.* He was the one who advised his followers not "Go for the gold!" but rather, "The greatest among you must become like the youngest, and the leader like one who serves" (Lk 22:26). Jesus not only said this but did this, modeling a strange, countercultural leadership style with basin and towel.

Craig Hill marshals his vast erudition of the New Testament to show how early Christian views on status and ambition are some of the most interesting, demanding, and uniquely Christian practices. It might be possible for someone to argue that Jesus taught good old common sense, that the way of Christ is not too different from the American way, and that the church is similar to most other human gatherings. But then comes the New Testament and early Christian communities' attempts to embody those teachings—on the perils of measuring self-worth by status and the dangers of giving one's life to the demands of ambition. And even the most complacent mind knows that it has come to a head-on collision with conventional practice.

The section of the book on ambition and status among bishops made a hierarch like me deeply, irrevocably—yet salubriously—uncomfortable.

Craig shows how New Testament authors used theology to form and sustain a distinctive community, and to equip and to encourage believers to get along with each other, especially where differing social status created an impediment to full fellowship in Jesus' name. In spite of the status-grubbing values of the surrounding Roman culture, these fledgling churches dared to work toward "having the same love, being in full accord and of one mind" (Phil 2:2b).

Church is not where we come to burnish our own status and honor. Church is a place where our ambitiousness and status consciousness must be faithfully examined. Be prepared to be enlisted in that adventure through reading this book.

Welcome to Craig Hill's wide-ranging mind. Craig enlists Tony Campolo, *The King and I*, Ron Heifetz, *The African Queen*, neuroscience, Jane Goodall, Malcolm Gladwell, the Apostle Paul, Crosby, Stills, Nash & Young, and lower primates to make his points. Throughout, *Servant of All* shows Craig's lifelong love of, commitment to, and service in behalf of the church. His decades of leadership in theological education, teaching pastors and seminarians how to lead in the manner of the New Testament, have enabled Craig to produce a very wise, imminently practical book that will equip readers to talk in more informed ways about issues of status and ambition in light of Scripture. Pastors and congregations will be shown how to be more faithful in their life together.

Servant of All will elevate Craig Hill's status as one of our premier New Testament scholars who writes in service to the church and its leaders even as the book checks some of my ambition and puts a much-needed leash on some of my status-seeking. What a great service Dean Craig Hill has rendered the church.

WILLIAM H. WILLIMON
Professor of the Practice of Christian Ministry,
  Duke Divinity School
United Methodist Bishop, retired

An Ironic Thing Happened on the Way to Publication

They say that God has a sense of humor. That might well be true.

I wrote this book while serving as a professor at Duke Divinity School. I was entering what I expected to be the last decade of my active career, having worked for over thirty years in churches, universities, and seminaries. My wife, Robin, and I were happily settled in Durham, North Carolina, and anticipated remaining there for our eventual retirement.

My central responsibility at Duke was creating and then administering its Doctor of Ministry Program. Through it, I got to know scores of exceptional pastors and other church professionals, many of them in mid-career. It quickly became apparent that, like the rest of us, they struggled with the desire for appreciation and acceptance. It was out of our many conversations that this book was born, and it is to them that it is dedicated.

A few weeks after writing the concluding chapter, I was contacted by an executive search firm, asking me to consider applying for the deanship of Perkins School of Theology at Southern Methodist University in Dallas, Texas. As I got to know the school, reluctance gave way to interest and ultimately to enthusiasm. I came to regard their invitation as a potential call to which I should be open. As you will have guessed, I was offered and then accepted the job. As you might imagine, that put me in an awkward and rather humorous position, having just written a book on the subject of status and ambition. It was a bit safer tackling this topic from one of the back rows. Moreover, the book made a few explicit references to seminary deans. Rather than expunge these, I retained them as an inside joke offered at my own expense. Never in my wildest dreams did it occur to me as I wrote that these might be taken to be self-referential!

I do have one concern. The last thing I want readers to take away from this book is the notion that Christian faithfulness and worldly advancement walk hand in hand. To the contrary, I believe they are at least as often at odds. Indeed, each advancement carries with it new temptations to unfaithfulness. As a form of power, recognition may easily corrupt, all the more subtly if it is offered up by the church. Knowing this, I have come to see this book as written especially for me—and only then, by extension, for other fallible human beings who seek to please God without deceiving themselves.

CRAIG C. HILL
Perkins School of Theology
Dallas, Texas

ACKNOWLEDGMENTS

Duke Divinity School, which gave me the time to write this book.

Judith Heyhoe, who provided invaluable editorial assistance.

Rev. Scott Anderson and the congregation of St. Paul's Lutheran Church in Durham, North Carolina, who provided the office where I wrote most of what follows.

Members of the Genesis Class at Epworth United Methodist Church in Durham, North Carolina, who read and responded to the initial draft of several chapters.

Robin, my splendid wife, who daily models the virtues described in this book.

CHAPTER ONE

"The Best of Disinfectants"

Status is not a gift of the Spirit.[1] Ambition is absent from lists of spiritual fruit in the New Testament.[2] Authority, honor, and rank are at best ambiguous scriptural categories. Still, Christians remain ambitious, desire status, and seek higher stations. Are they wrong?

In over two decades spent training Christian leaders, I have found no constellation of issues so seldom discussed and yet of such intense interest. Clergy may more comfortably converse about their sexuality or mental health than about their own need for recognition and affirmation. This need, if they are honest, was part of their motivation for entering the ministry and is much of what makes remaining in it difficult. Invite this conversation, however, and a lively, even liberating, exchange ensues. It is a relief not to have to pretend that we are unconcerned with our standing. Better to expose our veiled aspirations and attempt to think openly and faithfully about them. As Supreme Court Justice Louis D. Brandeis put it, "Sunlight is . . . the best of disinfectants."

The relative inattention given this issue has been, at least until fairly recently, paralleled in my own academic field, New

---

1. Cf. 1 Cor 12:8–10. Unless otherwise noted, biblical quotations are taken from the New Revised Standard Version.
2. Cf. Gal 5:22–23.

Testament studies.[3] This oversight is perfectly understandable. Scholars read the Bible for its theology, and theologians love big ideas: Salvation History, the Holy Trinity, and the Kingdom of God. They spend years constructing grand theoretical edifices: the Documentary Hypothesis, the Apocalyptic Perspective, and the Historical Jesus. Life is an adventure, and there is nothing more intellectually adventurous than the quest for original answers to great questions.

Indisputably, the New Testament is a rich repository of profound theological concepts. What is often overlooked, however, is the fact that its authors did not write theology for theology's sake. Typically, theological ideas were enlisted in support of practical aims. The work that theology was required to do varied. It might provide encouragement to believers in a time of distress (Revelation), or it might explain why certain religious practices had been either adopted or abandoned (Galatians). Often, theology was called upon to assist in the pedestrian but still urgent task of helping believers to get along with each other.

Some of the most prominent New Testament churches were comprised of an unconventional and unwieldy admixture of slaves and masters, Jews and Gentiles, women and men, educated and illiterate, as well as highborn and lowly. All natural human tendencies toward hierarchy, segregation, and factionalism were encouraged by this diversity and by the fact that these communities were something new, without established structures or clear precedents. What held them together? How were they to regard and to organize themselves, and how were they to behave in each other's company? These matters had to be resolved, and the resolutions offered were typically grounded in theology. The hoped-for conse-

3. Led by several prominent scholars, including E. A. Judge, Wayne Meeks, Jerome H. Neyrey, and Bruce Malina, the sociological/social-historical study of the New Testament has emerged in recent decades as an independent academic specialization. The present study, though written for a general audience and contributing nothing new to that discipline, owes much to it. For an introduction to this field of study, see, for example, Philip A. Harland, *Dynamics of Identity in the World of the Early Christians* (London: Continuum, 2009), 1–19.

quence was that the communities would understand themselves as existing in a new reality in which ordinary tendencies toward one-upmanship, strife, and division would seem unacceptable and would become aberrant.

Take for example the famous Christ Hymn of Phil 2:5b–11, often cited as a key text for the study of early Christology (the subject of Christ's identity):

> Christ Jesus, who, though he was in the form of God, did not count equality with God a thing to be grasped, but emptied himself, taking the form of a servant, being born in human likeness. (Phil 2:5b–7)

Cutting to the theological chase, we skip the entire preceding paragraph, which encourages the Philippian Christians to practice meekness and cooperation. The Christ Hymn is thus the conclusion to a rather everyday exhortation to humility and concord. It is in this context and with this prompting that Paul writes,

> *Have this mind among yourselves,* which is yours in Christ Jesus, who, though he was in the form of God . . . (Phil 2:5–6a)

Paul speaks elsewhere in the letter of rivalries and discord within the church (Phil 1:15–18; 4:2–3), without which he might never have inserted the extraordinary passage on the self-emptying of Jesus. The same pattern is found throughout the New Testament: *problems in human relationships necessitated theological reflection.*[4] Nevertheless, these reflections are often studied in isolation from their original function, which is comprehensible given that the primary concern of theologians is theology. Still, something is lost when these passages are pried free of their immediate purpose. In particular, the valuable lessons they provide today's

---

4. Joseph H. Hellerman aptly commented, "The grand narrative of Christ's humiliation and exaltation came alive for me anew when I recognized that Paul's designs in the passage were not primarily christological. They were ecclesiological." *Embracing Shared Ministry: Power and Status in the Early Church and Why It Matters Today* (Grand Rapids: Kregel, 2013), 11.

church can be missed by focusing only on the theology and not on the job the theology was created to do.

It is the aim of this short book to consider how New Testament authors used theology to form and sustain community—or, more basic still, to equip and encourage believers to get along with each other, especially where differing social status creates an impediment to fellowship. It is my hope that this study will help Christians today to approximate more nearly the vision of a church community "having the same love, being in full accord and of one mind" (Phil 2:2b).

I have chosen to focus exclusively on the New Testament for three reasons: 1) most readers will themselves be located in Christian churches, which are first described and modelled in the pages of the New Testament; 2) reviewing the whole of Scripture would result in a book of unmanageable length; and 3) New Testament is my field of study. The danger is that I will leave readers with the false impression that all that is good and noble in the New Testament is unprecedented in and unrelated to the Old Testament.[5] Nothing could be further from the truth, a point to which I shall occasionally return. Perhaps I—or, much better, someone with real expertise in the field of Old Testament studies—will extend this work in the future.

Status

The majority of this book is devoted to the subject of status, a ubiquitous factor and problem in human relationships throughout history, not least in the first century CE. As the Greek historian and biographer Plutarch observed nearly two millennia ago, the "love of fame, the desire to be first and greatest . . . is a disease most prolific of envy, jealousy, and discord."[6] Andrew D. Clarke of the University of Aberdeen summarized the situation in this way: "Graeco-

---

5. I do not advocate for a form of Marcionism, named for the second-century figure Marcion, who rejected the Old Testament.

6. Plutarch, *Mor.* 10.788E (Fowler, LCL).

Roman society was highly stratified, and at all levels of community life people recognized and elevated the *status quo* whereby those of comparatively greater rank and social standing received due deference and honour."[7] Consequently, it is not surprising that social distinctions were carried over into the early church, especially by its more prominent members, and that New Testament authors would counter breakdowns in Christian community by means of an alternative conceptualization of status, typically grounded in the example of Christ, as we have just seen in Phil 2.

This last statement compels me to acknowledge an unavoidable tension, highlighted by J. E. Lendon in his seminal work *Empire of Honour: The Art of Government in the Roman World.* Put one way, it is the fact that people who shun worldly distinction might for that very reason be celebrated. "Philosophers were doomed to be honoured for their scorn of honour."[8] There is no escaping the fact that the behavior of some persons is more praiseworthy than that of others. The New Testament singles out, for example, the exemplars of faith in Heb 11:4–38. True, but it should be added that the vast majority of those who labor humbly and faithfully are never adequately recognized for their service. The wife who lovingly sacrifices for her terminally ill husband and the man who gives up a high-visibility, high-paying job to work for a non-profit will not see statues erected in their honor. Public acclaim is a fickle companion and a terrible master.[9]

7. Andrew D. Clarke, *Serve the Community of the Church: Christians as Leaders and Ministers* (Grand Rapids: Eerdmans, 2000), 146–47.

8. J. E. Lendon, *Empire of Honour: The Art of Government in the Roman World* (Oxford: Oxford University Press, 1997), 91.

9. Most challenging to me personally is Lendon's quotation from Cicero: "philosophers inscribe their own names on those very books in which they write that glory should be scorned" (*Empire of Honour*, 92). Should a book such as this be published anonymously? In fact, it has been done. A student who read my manuscript brought to my attention the following: *Embracing Obscurity: Becoming Nothing in Light of God's Everything* by "Anonymous" (Nashville: Broadman & Holman, 2012). Ironically but perhaps inevitably, given the needs of publishers, the book contains pages of named endorsements. I admire what I take to be the author's sincere choice. At the same time, I believe that readers should evaluate a book in context, which includes knowing who wrote it, "warts and all."

Lendon goes on to say that "Christian views of honour offered the starkest possible challenge to aristocratic pagan attitudes."[10] Nevertheless, in practice the church developed its own honor system. That is not necessarily a bad thing, depending in part on the what, how, how much, and why of the honoring. But it was inherently dangerous. In time, the worlds of public and ecclesial honor merged, with aristocrats becoming bishops, who "cultivated their reputations, [and] were furious if they were not treated appropriately to their high social position, and adopted the insignia and garb of the highest Roman dignitaries." In short, these "Christian aristocrats were more aristocratic than Christian."[11]

As we shall see, the problem did not take centuries to emerge. It was there at the beginning, albeit in less blatant form. Existing status systems were readily imported into the church, and it took great effort and ingenuity on the part of the New Testament authors to challenge them.

Ambition

The subtitle of this book lists ambition alongside status. While a worthy subject in itself, it is treated here as a subsidiary issue, dealt with primarily in chapter 8. Ambition would be far less problematic were it not for its close kinship to status. (The same can be said for hierarchy, which is the subject of chapter 9.) Someone is disparaged as "overly ambitious" because she is thought to be self-promoting. A candidate vies for a top spot in the political hierarchy but is careful to say that he is motivated by love of country—and not, implicitly, by love of adulation. Truly, "there is nothing new under the sun" (Eccl 1:9). Another first-century Roman, the philosopher Dio Chrysostom, criticized those who seek high office:

> Not for the sake of what is truly best and in the interest of their country itself, but for the sake of reputation and honours and

10. Lendon, *Empire of Honour,* 92.
11. Lendon, *Empire of Honour,* 95.

the possession of greater power than their neighbours, in the pursuit of crowns and precedence and purple robes, fixing their gaze upon these things and staking all upon their attainment, do and say such things as will enhance their own reputations.[12]

We might well ask ourselves what work we would be ambitious to do if no one else could know about it.

As we shall see, ambition, like status, is an equivocal category, neither inherently good nor bad, something both hard to live with and hard to live without. It is noteworthy that the New Testament most often treats ambition as problematic when it is associated with status, as it so very often is.

These matters are of relevance to all Christians, whether Protestant or Catholic, liberal or conservative, clergy or laity, famous or obscure. For that reason, I set to one side divisive issues that do not require resolution. A primary example is the approach taken in chapters 3 and 4 to the Gospels. Our chief concern is how the Gospel writers, Mark in particular, hoped to influence the behavior of their contemporary readers. This does not necessitate that we settle contentious issues of authorship and dating, much less that we sort through layers of tradition and justify this or that saying as historically authentic. Such a study would be at least five times as long and, I venture, one-tenth as useful. I flag matters of scholarly debate occasionally, but in no case is agreement with me expected, much less required. In short, let us not forget that what Scripture has to say on these points is of consequence to us all. Before approaching the New Testament, however, we need to consider the nature of the problem. Why do these issues arise at all, and how might we begin to frame a Christian understanding of them?

---

12. Dio Chrysostom, *2 Tars. (Or. 34)* 29 (Thayer, LCL).

CHAPTER TWO

It's Only Natural

Innumerable stories, both dramas and comedies, rely on the pairing of opposites. Persons of contrasting backgrounds and viewpoints are thrown together by chance. Sparks fly, but in time the adversaries learn to appreciate—and, in the case of romances, to love—each other. This is the setup for countless novels, most eminently Jane Austen's *Pride and Prejudice*, and for movies as varied as *In the Heat of the Night, The Odd Couple, Toy Story,* and *Men in Black.*

It is also the plot device of the classic film *The African Queen.* Humphrey Bogart plays Charlie Allnut, an earthy, rough-hewn, and hard-drinking captain of the ship. His accidental foil is Rose Sayer (Katharine Hepburn), a rigid and indomitable Methodist missionary. At one point, Charlie awakens from a drunken stupor to see Rose pouring his remaining bottles of gin overboard. "And you call yourself a Christian! . . . What you being so mean for, Miss? A man takes a drop too much once in a while. It's only human nature." Rose haughtily retorts, "Nature, Mr. Allnut, is what we were put in this world to rise above."

The story does not end there. Over the remainder of the film, the two protagonists come to see the best in each other, and sparks of a different sort fly. In the end, they are united in marriage, and their personalities and perspectives meet in the middle. Charlie curbs his "natural" inclinations, and Rose realizes that all natural pleasures are not evil.

8

Christianity contains within itself a comparable clash of opposing perspectives. One side regards natural longings as unspiritual and so best subjugated and left unexpressed. Hence, ascetics of all ages have attempted to free themselves from fleshly impulse. The opposite extreme is to assume that whatever is natural is, by that definition, good—or at least of no spiritual consequence. This is one of several errors the apostle Paul challenged in his fledgling church at Corinth. If we are freed from the Jewish Law, some reasoned, we are at liberty to do with our bodies as our bodies please (1 Cor 6:13). How we use our bodies might not save us, Paul reasoned, but it still matters, affecting us both physically and spiritually (1 Cor 6:15–18).

Between Repression and Indulgence

Most contemporary Christians would have little trouble accepting the idea that their faith ought to play a role in regulating natural drives. The obvious example is sex. An enormous amount of attention has been given in recent decades to the rehabilitation of sex as a God-given gift. Few today would advocate either total repression of sexual instinct or, at the other extreme, total capitulation to the vagaries of sexual desire. Instead, the focus is on drawing the line between healthful and destructive (and thus sinful) sexual behavior. Intense debate rages over the question of where that line is to be drawn, but it is noteworthy that nearly all sides agree on the fundamental premise: sexual desire is natural and, channeled appropriately, good.

A second and perhaps equally fixated-upon impulse is hunger. To survive, humans need not only to procreate; they need to eat. Eating, like sex, is naturally pleasurable, a fact that generates the same contrasting responses. Throughout history, some have denied themselves the joys of good eating for the sake of spiritual attainment. The purest expression is fasting, often commended as a spiritual discipline and sometimes practiced by Jesus himself. But how far is too far? Is one living on the edge of self-imposed starvation pleasing God?

On the other side of the ledger are those who seem oblivious to the sin of gluttony, to both the physical and spiritual effects of self-indulgence. This is a bit too close for comfort: it is not unusual for pastors to be more overweight and less healthy than the general population. Is the credibility of one's preaching undermined by what appears at least to be a capitulation to raw animal instinct? "What you being so mean for? A person takes a bite too much once in a while. It's only human nature."[1] Can we not agree at least that our faith ought to give us a way of thinking about the consumption of food that is life-giving, that "honors God in our bodies" (1 Cor 6:20), without being either ascetic or intemperate?

We may extend this discussion to the emotions. Strictly speaking, emotions are natural since they are mediated by and experienced in our physical bodies. My father died fairly recently. I am grateful that I do not have to pretend that my natural feelings of grief are evil. Jesus himself displayed altogether human emotions (e.g., Mark 9:19; 15:34). At the same time, we ought not to be slaves to our emotions. The heart (much less the reptilian brain) can and sometimes does lead us astray.[2] Neither romantic love nor righteous anger is an adequate legal or moral defense.

Already we see a paradigm emerging. Natural drives are basic and necessary to human existence.[3] Religion has from time to time gone off the rails by attempting to quash those impulses entirely. This way of thinking is most common in what are called

1. To be fair, it is not a level playing field. People are more or less likely to gain weight depending on factors other than how much they eat. What they eat (especially carbohydrates) matters a lot, as does their body's level of insulin production and insulin resistance, among other factors. See Gary Taubes, *Why We Get Fat: And What to Do About It* (New York: Alfred A. Knopf, 2011).

2. The term (also known as the R-Complex) refers to the basal ganglia, tissue at the brain's base associated with, among other things, emotion.

3. On the relationship between biology, ethics, and religious faith, see Philip Clayton, "Biology and Purpose: Altruism, Morality, and Human Nature in Evolutionary Perspective," in *Evolution and Ethics: Human Morality in Biological and Religious Perspective*, ed. Philip Clayton and Jeffrey Schloss (Grand Rapids: Eerdmans, 2004), 318–36. Much of what Clayton writes would be of relevance even to Christians who challenge the theory of evolution.

"dualistic systems," which regard nature (or "flesh") and spirit as absolute and irreconcilable opposites. We are thus spiritual to the extent that we overcome nature. The ideal would be to separate ourselves from the body entirely and live as pure spirits. There are many problems with this way of thinking, not least the simple fact that we are embodied creatures who, however much we might try, *cannot* live outside of our physical beings. How often must we hear news accounts of church leaders who propagate an otherworldly gospel but who secretly indulge in sexual misconduct? It is dangerous to pretend that we exist above the natural world. We live in nature, and it is in nature, in the body, that God meets us in Jesus Christ.

On the opposite side of the road lies another, equally hazardous ditch: the assertion that whatever is natural is self-evidently justified. Did not God create nature itself and pronounce it good (Gen 1:31)? Indeed, Nature with a capital "N" is used as a virtual synonym for God. The difficulty is that nature is deeply ambiguous. One can locate natural occurrences of almost any behavior. A mother dog might raise an abandoned kitten along with her pups. On the other hand, a grown male cat might kill a rival's litter. Which behavior is natural, altruism or infanticide? Moreover, left unchecked, instincts that help to preserve the species can also destroy it. Grazing is good, but overgrazing leads to starvation.

Because of our intelligence, inventiveness, and technology, such ambiguities are pressed to extremes in humans. Violent behavior might be natural amongst chimpanzees, but its effects are limited. That is not the case with humans, who possess the means to eliminate terrestrial life with the push of a button. But humans also possess capacities of self-awareness and self-determination that far exceed those of other animals. That makes us moral agents in a way that, say, Komodo dragons are not. And "to whom much is given, much will be required" (Luke 12:48).

I recall a television documentary in which an expert cited the behavior of a promiscuous bird species as justification for her own sexual infidelity. Her comment reminded me of "The Song of the King" from the Rogers and Hammerstein musical *The King and I*.

King Mongkut of Siam, a role owned by Yul Brynner, justified his polygamy by citing the example of the bee, flitting from flower to flower:

> A girl must be like a blossom
> With honey for just one man.
> A man must be like honey bee
> And gather all he can.
> To fly from blossom to blossom
> A honey bee must be free,
> But blossom must not ever fly
> From bee to bee to bee.

So much for the birds and the bees. In fact, one could rationalize almost any behavior in this way. Hence, it is not enough to say that an act "is only natural." But neither is it fully true that we are able "to rise above nature." Instead, the truth lies somewhere between, as both Charlie Allnut and Rose Sayer came to discover.

Lions and Tigers and Bears . . .
and Dolphins and Baboons and Kangaroos

The social life of animals is endlessly fascinating, as demonstrated by the fame of Jane Goodall's pioneering field study of chimpanzees and witnessed in the popularity of the television series *Meerkat Manor*. The reason is surely the many parallels we draw between animal relationships and the dramas and antics of human communities. While one must guard against projecting human emotions and motivations onto animals, scientists increasingly recognize that humans are not the only creatures to inhabit a lively and complex social world.

That many animals live in groups is easily taken for granted. In fact, such behavior represents a remarkable adaptation. The benefits of group functioning are considerable, including diversification of roles (such as worker and soldier ants), protection against predators (one animal serves as a lookout), increased food gathering capacity (the group searches a broader range), assistance with rearing offspring (others care for the young while the parent forages), and social support (play and grooming).

There are costs as well as benefits, both to the group and to its individual members. Some risks, such as starvation and disease, are amplified in a community setting. Most animal societies exhibit a dominance hierarchy, which means that its benefits are not distributed equally. The alternative, however, can be near-constant disorder, competition, and strife, making the entire herd, pack, flock, troop, or pride less productive and more vulnerable. The form animal hierarchies takes varies enormously, but their existence across so many species is both undeniable and worthy of our attention.

In his seminal work *Leadership without Easy Answers*, Ronald A. Heifetz of Harvard University outlines the similarities and differences between gorilla and chimpanzee societies. He then lists five functions performed by the dominant individual(s) of both species:

1. Choosing the direction of group movement
2. Protecting the group from predators
3. Orienting members to their status and place
4. Controlling conflict
5. Maintaining norms, including norms of mating and resource allocation[4]

This comes eerily close to being the job description of a seminary dean.

Although most such studies focus on primates, a similar list could be drawn up from observations of the lives of other social animals, such as wolves, kangaroos, badgers, goats, horses, hyenas, and pigs. As we might expect, physical size often plays a major role in establishing rank, but other factors trump brute strength in some animals. For example, age, not body mass, typically de-

---

4. Ronald A. Heifetz, *Leadership Without Easy Answers* (Cambridge: Harvard University Press, 1994), 53.

termines relative status amongst female bottlenose dolphins[5] and beef cattle.[6] Also, group boundaries are often fluid. A gorilla unhappy with the current silverback might seek out a different band under more congenial leadership. Moreover, movement up and down animal hierarchies is common, although disruption of the established order carries a cost to the entire society. Too much instability and group cohesion disintegrates. Status conflicts, especially between mature males, can be deadly, most notably in clashes over mating rights. In many species, however, these conflicts involve mostly ritualistic displays—such as an alpha wolf showing its teeth—which minimize the danger to both the individuals and the group. Male orangutans are especially well adapted to avoid unnecessary conflict. In any single location, only one male becomes fully mature, developing distinctive secondary sexual characteristics, e.g., those marvelously large cheek pads. Others remain in a juvenile state until the dominant male is dead or displaced, at which point the largest juvenile takes the leading role, morphing into a mature male over a matter of months.[7]

We would be right to assume that a position of dominance carries with it many advantages. Animals at the top of the pecking order typically eat better, reproduce more, are more frequently and better groomed, have more opportunities to vent aggression, and, in some species at least, are safer. The opposite is true for individuals at the bottom. Those animals are more likely to live on the periphery of the group, putting them in greater danger, to work harder, to eat less, and to mate more seldom, if ever. Perhaps most significant is the fact that they live under greater stress, which inhibits "digestion, growth, tissue repair, and reproduction."[8] Chronic stress suppresses the immune system and makes an ani-

5. Amy Samuels and Tara Gifford, "A Quantitative Assessment of Dominance Relations among Bottlenose Dolphins," *Marine Mammal Science* 13.1 (1997): 70–99.

6. Radka Šárová, Marek Špinka, et al., "Pay Respect to the Elders: Age, More than Body Mass, Determines Dominance in Female Beef Cattle," *Animal Behaviour* 86.6 (2013): 1315–23.

7. Robert M. Sapolsky, "Social Status and Health in Humans and Other Animals," *Annual Review of Anthropology* 33 (2004): 393–418 (402).

8. Sapolsky, "Social Status and Health in Humans and Other Animals," 394.

mal more susceptible to a range of maladies, including infectious diseases, peptic ulcers, high blood pressure, and heart disease.[9] Strikingly, one study of stress found that "the pattern of changes in a subordinate baboon was identical to what occurs in humans with major depression."[10] We are not the only ones who get down in the dumps from being on the losing end of social encounters.

The relationship between social rank and stress has been studied extensively. For example, it has been shown that high-status baboons in stable hierarchies have smaller adrenal glands and exhibit lower blood levels of the stress hormone cortisol.[11] The situation changes markedly, however, in times of social instability. If the dominant individual is repeatedly challenged, especially by a near equal, its stress level rises precipitously. The same is not true for lower-placed individuals who win such contests. In other words, it is not so much the instability itself as the meaning of the instability to a particular individual that determines whether or not it is stressful.

Several factors govern the amount of stress experienced by animals. Stress is minimized when one exercises a significant degree of control over one's circumstances, when those circumstances are predictable, when one experiences sufficient social support, and when outlets exist for potentially disruptive emotions such as anger and frustration.[12] Not coincidentally, this list correlates closely with studies of human job satisfaction.[13] A micromanaging boss, a company shakeup, and an impersonal work

9. Jay R. Kaplan, Stephen B. Manuck, et al., "Social Status, Environment, and Atherosclerosis in Cynomolgus Monkeys," *Arteriosclerosis, Thrombosis, and Vascular Biology* 2 (1982): 359–68.

10. Sapolsky, "Social Status," 399.

11. Robert M. Sapolsky, "The Endocrine Stress-Response and Social Status in the Wild Baboon," *Hormones and Behavior* 16.3 (1982): 279–92.

12. Robert M. Sapolsky, "Cortisol Concentrations and the Social Significance of Rank Instability among Wild Baboons," *Psychoneuroendocrinology* 17.6 (1992): 701–9 (702).

13. See, for example, J. R. Hackman and G. R. Oldham, "How Job Characteristics Theory Happened," in *The Great Minds in Management: The Process of Theory Development*, ed. Ken G. Smith and Michael A. Hitt (Oxford: Oxford University Press, 2005), 151–70.

environment all elevate stress and create the same kinds of physical responses in us as experienced by our evolutionary cousins living under roughly parallel circumstances.

The Human Experience

Our hunter-gatherer forebearers might well have experienced fewer social stresses, living in small, mobile and relatively egalitarian groups. (Environmental stressors more than made up for it, we would suppose.) The invention of agriculture profoundly changed all that. Cultivation of land and domestication of animals required that groups locate in a particular place. They also made possible much larger population concentrations and, with them, an increased division of labor. Hamlets became villages, villages became cities, and clusters of cities became nation-states. Along the way, human societies became increasingly stratified and hierarchical.

Scientists are only beginning to understand the amazing extent to which the human brain is wired socially. Writes David Rock,

> This social network is something we're born with. Newborn babies orient toward a picture of a face, above any other picture, when just a few minutes old. At six months, well before they can speak, infants experience advanced socially oriented emotions such as jealousy.[14]

The brain devotes considerable resources to determining one's place in the group. "Maintaining high status is something that the brain seems to work on all the time subconsciously."[15] Increases in status release rewards of serotonin, dopamine, and testosterone.[16]

14. David Rock, *Your Brain at Work: Strategies for Overcoming Distraction, Regaining Focus, and Working Smarter All Day Long* (New York: Harper Business, 2009), 158.

15. Rock, *Your Brain at Work*, 193.

16. Unsurprisingly, the extent to which this is the case varies from person to person and is to a significant extent determined by physiology. On variations in

The opportunity to increase status is therefore a potent motivator. People are willing to make extraordinary sacrifices in the hope of winning acclaim.

The desire to avoid diminished status is an equal, perhaps even more formidable, influence. Threats to status are perceived by the brain in the same way as threats to survival, and drops in status are processed in the same regions of the brain as those associated with physical suffering.[17] In many cultures, including that of the ancient Greco-Roman world, the threat of shame was an especially potent sanction. Crucifixion, a penalty reserved primarily for slaves, was imposed upon those whom the Roman state wished to humiliate utterly.[18] Chester Nez, in his autobiography *Code Talkers,* wrote of his experience facing Japanese soldiers in World War II who preferred suicide to capture, which would shame both them and their families. In a warrior culture, death on behalf of the Empire brings honor,[19] a perspective similar to that of today's suicide bombers. We who regard these as extreme examples are nevertheless careful to avoid situations that might jeopardize our status, especially in the presence of strangers or higher-status persons. In short, status is an inescapable factor that profoundly affects every human life.

Fortunately for us, complex communities contain an array of status systems. Students who struggle in the classroom might win attention through humor or sports. The old adage that one's home is one's castle gets at the same reality. A lowly, overlooked employee can be the family's anchor and center. This same lesson is conveyed in many popular films, most famously the Frank Capra classic *It's a Wonderful Life.* A more recent movie of this genre, *The Family Man,* centers on the character of Jack Campbell (Nicolas

"reward sensitivity," see Susan Cain, *Quiet: The Power of Introverts in a World That Can't Stop* Talking (New York: Broadway Books, 2012), 157–61.

17. Rock, *Your Brain at Work,* 105, 189–90; specifically, the dorsal portion of the anterior cingulate cortex.

18. See Wenhua Shi, *Paul's Message of the Cross as Body Language,* WUNT 2.254 (Tübingen: Mohr Siebeck, 2008), 20–52 ("Crucifixion in Antiquity").

19. Chester Nez, with Judith Schiess Avila, *Code Talker* (New York: Berkeley Books, 2011), 141.

Cage), who wants to pursue a lucrative career on Wall Street that would force his family to abandon its settled, happy life in suburban New Jersey. He tells his wife, Kate (Téa Leoni), "Don't you see? I'm talking about us finally having a life that other people envy." "Oh, Jack," she replies, "they already do envy us." There are many ways of being somebody in today's world, and an abject failure by one measure can be a stunning success by another.

Our senses receive approximately eleven million bits of information every second, but they are capable of processing only about forty bits per second.[20] It is out of those forty bits that our brains construct our perceived reality. That is why two people can experience the same situation in diametrically opposite ways: they collect different data and so draw a remarkably different mental picture. The encouraging news is that we are active partners in this process and can, at least to an extent, choose the information on which to focus. Those who are adept at seeing opportunity where others see only obstruction and failure are among the most valuable assets of any organization.[21]

Finding Our Place in the World

Our ability to conceptualize creates almost limitless options as we consider our place in the world. Who we think ourselves to be—and what others think us to be—is not simply a function of, say, our physical size or testosterone and estrogen levels, although such attributes do profoundly affect us. We are situated within multiple, often overlapping communities. Some of these—such as our family, ethnic group, and social class—are given at birth. A multiplicity of other social groupings is entered—whether by the action of others, by accident, or by our own choice—over a lifetime. It is in large part through these myriad interactions and experiences that

20. Manfred Zimmerman, "Neurophysiology of Sensory Systems," in *Fundamentals of Sensory Physiology*, ed. Robert F. Schmidt, 3rd rev. ed. (New York: Springer, 1986), 31–80.

21. Shawn Achor, *Before Happiness: 5 Actionable Strategies to Create a Positive Path to Success* (New York: Random House, 2013), 25–27.

we construct an identity, and with it, one hopes, a positive sense of purpose and meaning, a feeling of place and belonging.

Context matters. In his book *David and Goliath: Underdogs, Misfits, and the Art of Battling Giants,* Malcolm Gladwell compared the bottom third of math and science students at Harvard University with the top third at a lower ranked school, Hartwick College.[22] Only a tiny percentage of the bottom-tier Harvard students graduated in those demanding fields, while the great majority of those in the highest-ranked group at Hartwick survived and even thrived. Here's the rub: those Harvard students had shown more aptitude than the best students at the lesser school. Whether one was encouraged or discouraged to stick it out, in other words, had more to do with context than with ability. Writes Gladwell, "What matters . . . is not just how smart you are. It's how smart you *feel* relative to the other people in your classroom."[23] It is often more affirming to be a big fish in a small pond than the reverse.

I witnessed the same thing as a student and then college chaplain at Oxford University. With respect to status, the high point of the whole experience was being admitted. In my context in Peoria, Illinois, that was exciting news. Once you arrive on the scene, however, you are in the same boat as everyone else. It is no big deal to be an Oxford student in Oxford. Indeed, for some it is quite stressful and even depressing. Many who were accustomed to being top performers are suddenly just average. I witnessed this phenomenon most poignantly as a chaplain. I recall in particular two tragic suicides within the university community. By any reasonable measure, these young people were already highly successful with everything to live for, but that is not how things can appear in such a competitive environment.

Especially helpful for understanding self-perception is the concept of "the significant other."[24] Significant others are those

22. Malcolm Gladwell, *David and Goliath: Underdogs, Misfits, and the Art of Battling Giants* (New York: Little, Brown and Company, 2013), 81–86.

23. Gladwell, *David and Goliath*, 84.

24. Anthony Campolo, Jr., provides a helpful introduction to the concept of the significant other in *The Success Fantasy* (Wheaton: Victor Books, 1980),

whose opinion of us we solicit and believe. Ordinarily, parents are the first to fill this role. This is one reason why early abandonment by a parent can be so devastating. Many of us continue to take cues from our parents throughout our lives—directly, while they live, and through their internalized voice after they are gone. Over time, others are included in our circle of significance, whether a supportive teacher or the infamous adolescent peer group. As someone put it, "Who signs your report card?" Whose opinion of you most influences your opinion of yourself? Woe to those who spend their lives attempting to please the impossible to please. I once heard a renowned person confess that she was a lifelong "approval junkie." (Whose approval she had ever failed to win was not disclosed.) We shall return to the concept of the significant other in the next chapter.

Understandably, we all tend to value and invest in those status systems in which we ourselves excel. One of the most vital jobs of adolescence and young adulthood is the identification of one's gifts and thus of one's potential role. Ideally, finding a meaningful place to use our talents allows us to recognize and appreciate the talents of others. Of course, a yawning chasm divides ideal from actual human life. It is a rare organization of any size that does not experience tension, if not open conflict, around matters of status, often under the guise of other, more seemingly legitimate concerns. The argument at church over worship music might have more to do with a group's loss of status and influence than about the placement of a drum kit at the front of the sanctuary. Not that churches are especially culpable. With the possible exception of the military, is any institution more rank conscious than the modern university? It is not without reason that C. S. Lewis wrote the following sentence after his many years teaching at Oxford and Cambridge Universities:

> We must picture Hell as a state where everyone is perpetually concerned about his own dignity and advancement, where ev-

---

20–25. I recently reread the book and was struck by how much influence it has had over my own thinking for more than three decades.

eryone has a grievance, and where everyone lives the deadly serious passions of envy, self-importance, and resentment.[25]

Terms such as "rank," "status," "domination," and "submission," while of relevance, do not do justice to the complexity of human relationships and human self-understanding. We do not just experience our situation; we think about it, and our conceptual abilities allow us to think about it in almost limitless ways. Thus, the poor are capable of imagining themselves truly rich, and the rich truly poor. What's more, in religion we consider the place, not just of the individual in society, but of humanity itself in the wider universe.

We are meaning-seeking creatures, and it is within us to locate purpose in something more profound than our résumé or pocketbook. One might argue that this is simply misdirected biological drive. But perhaps our biology is meant to drive us to God. As Huston Smith put it,

> Built into the human makeup is a longing for a "more" that the world of everyday experience cannot requite. This outreach strongly suggests the existence of the something that life reaches *for* in the way that the wings of birds point to the reality of air. Sunflowers bend in the direction of light because light exists, and people seek food because food exists.[26]

Our hunger for meaning does not itself create meaning, but it might well be evidence that we are meant for something, for Someone, higher. Trying to live with the conviction that life is meaningless is like attempting to act without belief in free will: a pristine theory in constant collision with everyday human experience.[27] According to Simone Weil,

25. C. S. Lewis, *The Screwtape Letters* (New York: Macmillan, 1962), ix. This sentence is found in the preface to the British edition of 1961 and the American edition of 1962.

26. Huston Smith, *Why Religion Matters: The Fate of the Human Spirit in an Age of Disbelief* (San Francisco: HarperSanFrancisco, 2001), 3.

27. I refer the reader to William James's classic essay "The Dilemma of Deter-

A child does not stop crying if we suggest to it that perhaps there is no bread. It goes on crying just the same. The danger is not lest the soul should doubt whether there is any bread, but lest, by a lie, it should persuade itself that it is not hungry. It can only persuade itself of this by lying, for the reality of its hunger is not a belief, it is a certainty.[28]

In my role as a seminary professor, I have known hundreds of people who entered the ministry as a second career, sometimes at considerable cost, both financial and social. From the students' perspective, however, it was a worthwhile move, although a downward move by most calculations of status. They had bought—literally, in terms of lost revenue—into an alternative reality in which the less tangible gains outweighed the more evident losses. Note that this involved not the abandonment of place or purpose, but its redirection, its reconceptualization.

The easier course is to acquiesce to the prevailing status systems, especially if they treat us preferentially. Power, wealth and physical attractiveness are common denominators of status, which are displayed in everything from job titles to clothing styles, food preferences to street addresses. My favorite story about the ubiquity of status symbols was told by the wife of a pastor with whom I worked. Her husband was invited to preach at an unfamiliar church, and she went along and sat in the congregation.

minism." James concludes by saying that the belief that we may act freely to effect change "is what gives the palpitating reality to our moral life and makes it tingle ... with so strange and elaborate an excitement. This reality, this excitement, are what the determinisms, hard and soft alike, suppress by their denial that *anything* is decided here and now, and their dogma that all things were foredoomed and settled long ago. If it be so, may you and I then have been foredoomed to the error of continuing to believe in liberty. It is fortunate for the winding up of controversy that in every discussion with determinism this *argumentum ad hominem* can be its adversary's last word." William James, "The Dilemma of Determinism," *Unitarian Review and Religious Magazine*, 22.3 (1884): 193–224.

28. I found this quotation in Brian J. Mahan's stimulating book *Forgetting Ourselves on Purpose: Vocation and the Ethics of Ambition* (San Francisco: Jossey-Bass, 2002), 51. The original source is Simone Weil's *Waiting for God*, trans. Emma Craufurd (New York: HarperCollins, 1973), 210.

They knew the church was on the conservative end of the spectrum, but neither had realized in advance that this included the expectation that women would not wear jewelry (see 1 Pet 3:3). The unfortunate spouse eventually became aware of her breach and turned visibly uncomfortable. Just then, a perceptive elderly woman patted her on the knee and whispered, "That's all right, dear. We drive big cars."

Or consider our love of affiliation. We vicariously live through glamorous celebrities, and we exult or mourn with the fortunes of favorite sports teams. People come to blows over the most trivial of such allegiances, which do not seem at all trivial when one's identity is felt to be on the line. Coke or Pepsi, Ford or Chevy, Yankees or Red Sox?[29] Why does it matter? The fact that it can matter so much says a great deal about us.

Too Much of a Good Thing?

In an environment of scarcity, the ability to store excess energy as fat is an essential survival mechanism. This is especially true of the body's handling of simple carbohydrates, sugars and starches, which are not consistently available in many environments and which are quickly turned to fat. Scarcity was the common lot of our ancestors, especially early humans. It made sense to eat as much as they could whenever they could, especially high density calories that they could tuck away to see them through the inevitable lean times. Fast forward several millennia. For most readers of this book, the lean times never come. For those of us within easy driving distance of a supermarket, this formerly indispensable adaptation has become maladaptive. Our instinct has not caught up with our reality.

---

29. Even hobbies are riven by factions. Audiophiles divide into analog and digital camps, and hotly argue the case for objective or subjective equipment evaluation. Video gamers are adamant about the superiority of their platform, just as pinball enthusiasts have for years passionately debated the merits of electro-mechanical and solid-state machines. Ironically, those who share a common interest are often the most unyielding of combatants.

In particular, we consume quantities of carbohydrates that spike blood sugar. This spike tells the pancreas to release insulin, which rapidly lowers blood sugar causing us to crave more carbs—all of which makes us progressively fatter (a process called "reactive hypoglycemia"). We are programmed to enjoy such foods for a good reason, but that favorable arrangement backfires in an environment of superabundance. The answer is not a starvation diet but rather a balanced diet, one that provides the energy we need, that satisfies our hunger without promoting destructive cravings. Easier said than done, admits the man with a lifelong sweet tooth.

We can regard sex in much the same way. Where life expectancy is short and relationships unpredictable, it is understandable that a species would be promiscuous. The less that is the case—in other words, the less an environment of persistent danger and uncertainty exists—the more advantageous it becomes to form a lifelong commitment to a partner. Hence, it is not surprising that the idea of marriage exists across a wide range of advanced human cultures. And as we all know, the sex drive, essential to the propagation of the species, easily turns maladaptive, diminishing satisfaction and health—and damaging the wider society—even as it is indulged.

Likewise, the drive for status serves as a survival mechanism. In times of scarcity, one's rank in the herd can make the difference between life and death. Even more, it can determine the likelihood of passing one's genes on to the next generation. But the human race is not under threat of extinction, at least not from underpopulation. Most of us in the West live in comparative safety and relative abundance. We inhabit nations numbered in the millions of individuals, and the potential (all the more so now, thanks to the Internet) for finding a mate is comparatively high. For us, survival is rarely a matter of rank, and "status hunger" readily becomes maladaptive, its uncritical indulgence leading to less, not more, life satisfaction, and to countless social ills. We might well ask ourselves, what "status carbs" do we crave, and what might a balanced—not a starvation—diet contain?

Relationship to the New Testament

We started by considering the role of religion in channeling and regulating natural impulses. We saw that there are problematic alternatives on either side, whether in sweeping such matters under the rug, denying their importance, or in viewing these drives as unspiritual and therefore in need of vanquishing. We propose to think about the urge for status in much the same way as we think about sexual desire and hunger. It is a natural impulse, but it is ambiguous. We would do well neither to indulge nor to repress it. As with other such inclinations, we ought instead to attempt to think about it *Christianly*, to try to understand it within the context of our much wider understanding of reality.

For Christians, this is as much a corporate as it is an individual concern. We worship and have fellowship in groups, and those groups are of necessity organized. We know by now what that means: differentiation in labor, role and, inevitably, status. Whether this results in harmony and productivity or acrimony and impotence has everything to do with the way such a community is regarded by its members. How do faithful and effective Christian groups think about themselves? How are their resources, including their attention and care, distributed? At what points do they institutionalize the given social order, and at what points do they challenge it?

We would hope that the New Testament might have something to say about these matters, and indeed it does.[30] No human community floats innocently above these issues, and that includes the earliest churches. If anything, such concerns were amplified in these newly formed associations, many of which cut across received social hierarchies and barriers. They could well be regarded as a social laboratory. Would not such groups simply replicate existing hierarchies—and perhaps be destroyed by them? How

---

30. Please note the caveat found in the Introduction: I do not mean to imply that the Old Testament should not also be a source for Christian reflection. The New Testament did not arise *ex nihilo*, like Athena springing from the forehead of Zeus. It is a new link in an existing chain.

might they conceptualize a reality in which being together even makes sense?

There are no prepackaged answers to these questions, and so it is unsurprising that the New Testament authors addressed them in various ways. As we shall see, however, there is one element common to nearly every answer: an appeal to the example of Jesus.

CHAPTER THREE

The Example of Jesus

Now before the festival of the Passover, Jesus knew that his hour had come to depart from this world and go to the Father. Having loved his own who were in the world, he loved them to the end. . . . And during supper Jesus, knowing that the Father had given all things into his hands, and that he had come from God and was going to God, got up from the table, took off his outer robe, and tied a towel around himself. Then he poured water into a basin and began to wash the feet of the disciples and to wipe them with the towel that was tied around him.

(JOHN 13:1, 3–5)

Living in a culture in which a pair of Giuseppe Zanotti sandals sells for two thousand dollars, today's readers might well overlook the context assumed by this story. It would be more apparent to those living in the Arab world, where the foot is considered unclean. To show one's heel is an act of disrespect, and striking someone with a shoe is a sign of contempt.[1] Hence, recall the televised pictures in 2003 of crowds striking the fallen statue of Saddam Hussein with their footwear, followed five years later by the in-

---

1. Margo DeMello, *Feet and Footwear: A Cultural Encyclopedia* (Santa Barbara, CA: Macmillan, 2009), 205.

cident in which an Iraqi journalist threw his shoe at President George W. Bush.

In Jesus's day, social class was marked and reinforced in countless ways,[2] one of which was foot washing. It was a menial and dirty job, typically reserved for the lowest-ranking person in the house.

Ordinarily, the feet of guests would have been washed at their arrival, and so prior to a meal. That this had not happened in this story is telling. Throughout the Gospels, Jesus's disciples jostled with each other for position. It appears that they expected Jesus to go up to Jerusalem and be enthroned, fulfilling his messianic destiny. Like persons working in the inner circle of a presidential campaign, they imagined a day in the near future when they would ride the boss's coattails into high office. In consequence, they were inclined to see each other as rivals. So, for example, Mark 9:33–34:

> Then they came to Capernaum; and when he [Jesus] was in the house he asked them, "What were you arguing about on the way?" But they were silent, for on the way they had argued with one another about who was the greatest.

And Mark 10:35–37:

> James and John, the sons of Zebedee, came forward to him and said to him, "Teacher, we want you to do for us whatever we ask of you." And he said to them, "What is it you want me to do for you?" And they said to him, "Grant us to sit, one at your right hand and one at your left, in your glory."

The glory James and John sought was not of the heavenly variety. Perhaps earthly advancement was neither their initial nor their sole motive in following Jesus. Yet, it was a close companion on the journey and disunited them just as it disunites so many churches today.

---

2. On the issue of status in the Old Testament, see Ferdinand E. Deist, *The Material Culture of the Bible* (Sheffield: Sheffield Academic Press, 2000), 260–75.

We shall look at the disciples more closely in chapter 5, but for now it is enough to understand that each had a strategic reason not to become the designated foot washer. The one who did so would reinforce the others' good opinion of themselves and ensure his own inferior and servile status. The fact that Jesus's act occurred during supper, another breach of protocol, meant that it was a deliberate sign, a prophetic enactment, meant to make a point.

Most conspicuous is the use of the verb "to know." "Jesus *knew* that his hour had come to depart from this world and go to the Father . . . Jesus, *knowing* that the Father had given all things into his hands, and that he had come from God and was going to God" took up a towel. Jesus was the only one in the room who knew who he was, and thus the only one who was free to serve.

This story is followed in John 13:34–35 by the command to "love one another, even as I have loved you. . . . By this will all people know that you are my disciples, if you have love for one another." The kind of love Jesus required was modeled in the foot washing and would soon be fully demonstrated in his sacrificial death, which the foot washing foreshadowed (John 13:7).[3] As we shall see, the command to love and the call to serve heedless of social cost are often mentioned in the New Testament as evidence of the church's faithfulness and conditions of its fruitfulness. This short story contains a wealth of instruction on Christian living. Among other things, it shows how one might be attached to yet misaligned with Jesus. Like the disciples, we may be tempted to use Jesus as a new means to a decidedly old set of ends. It shows how fundamentally different was Jesus's own mindset, and it offers instruction on how his community of followers might emulate their master and, in so doing, get along with each other.

There is nothing in the Gospels about which scholars will ever agree fully—indeed, scholars make their living by disagreeing with

---

3. "It is not by chance that the washing of the feet comes at the beginning of the farewell discourses, since it points to Jesus's laying down his life." Reinhard Feldmeier, *Power, Service, Humility: A New Testament Ethic*, trans. Brian McNeil (Waco, TX: Baylor University Press, 2014), 48.

each other—and the jot-and-tittle historicity of this account is no exception. For example, there is dispute as to whether the original point of the story was to teach about humility (John 13:12–17) or the meaning of Jesus's death (cleansing from sin; John 13:6–11)—or both. Thankfully, such controversies need not occupy us here. The essential datum: this is how the early church remembered Jesus. Indeed, one matter about which the New Testament authors are most fully and firmly in agreement is the character of Jesus, concerning which John is only one vocalist in a chorus of witnesses.

The Mind of Jesus

Let's return briefly to the passage from Paul's letter to the church at Philippi mentioned in the Introduction:

> If then there is any encouragement in Christ, any consolation from love, any sharing in the Spirit, any compassion and sympathy, make my joy complete: be of the same mind, having the same love, being in full accord and of one mind. Do nothing from selfish ambition or conceit, but in humility regard others as better than yourselves. Let each of you look not to your own interests, but to the interests of others.
>
> Let the same mind be in you that was in Christ Jesus, who, though he was in the form of God, did not regard equality with God as something to be exploited ["grasped"], but emptied himself, taking the form of a slave, being born in human likeness. And being found in human form, he humbled himself and became obedient to the point of death— even death on a cross. Therefore God also highly exalted him and gave him the name that is above every name, so that at the name of Jesus every knee should bend, in heaven and on earth and under the earth, and every tongue should confess that Jesus Christ is Lord, to the glory of God the Father. (Phil 2:1–11)

Commentators focus on two issues in this passage: 1) did Paul believe in Christ's "pre-existence" (that Christ existed prior to his human birth; compare John 1:1–18); 2) is some or all of the second paragraph—known as the "Christ hymn" (Phil 2:5–11)—pre-Pauline, specifically, a piece of Christian poetry or hymnody quoted by Paul? The answer to both questions is probably "Yes," although neither conclusion is essential to our present study. However Paul imagined Christ's earlier life in God, it is obvious that he regarded his presence on Earth "in human form" as an act of self-emptying, which was perfected in a life of obedience and, ultimately, self-sacrifice. The addendum, "even death on a cross," is significant. Death by crucifixion was shameful and had been regarded by the pre-Christian Paul himself as evidence that Jesus was a false messiah, cursed by God (Gal 3:13). As we shall see in chapter 6, what had once been the center of Paul's unbelief became in time the very heart of his Christian faith. The cross gave Paul a fundamentally different understanding of God's presence in the world and so a fundamentally different way of evaluating his own life and calling.

Whether or not the Philippians already knew the words of the Christ hymn, Paul assumed that its characterization of Jesus would be accepted by them and so would validate his conclusion, namely, that his readers should behave humbly toward one another, not acting out of "selfish ambition or conceit," not prioritizing their own material self-interest.

The Love of Jesus

Echoing John 13, Paul in Phil 2 twice mentions love as the counter to these destructive impulses. For Paul, such love was exemplified in the cross: "God proves his love for us in that while we still were sinners Christ died for us" (Rom 5:8). A close parallel is 2 Cor 8:8b–9:

> I am testing the genuineness of your love. . . . For you know the generous act of our Lord Jesus Christ, that though he was rich, yet for your sakes he became poor, so that by his poverty you might become rich.

Again, the self-emptying of Jesus is the model of love. Paul has in mind here a specific application. He is asking the Corinthians to give generously to meet the needs of the churches in Judea. Like Christ, the Judean Christians had shared their abundant spiritual riches with the Corinthians, so it was only right that the Corinthians should now share their material wealth as an act of self-giving love toward "the saints" in Judea (9:1). Jesus's example is cited by Paul in a similar way in Rom 15:1–3:

> We who are strong ought to put up with the failings of the weak, and not to please ourselves. Each of us must please our neighbor for the good purpose of building up the neighbor. For Christ did not please himself; but, as it is written, "The insults of those who insult you have fallen on me."[4]

Much the same logic is found in 1 John 3:16–17:

> We know love by this, that he laid down his life for us—and we ought to lay down our lives for one another. How does God's love abide in anyone who has the world's goods and sees a brother or sister in need and yet refuses help?

"Laying down one's life" can occur in small acts of kindness as well as large acts of heroism. The great may even become the enemy of the good if we think that self-emptying for the sake of others is attainable only by the most saintly or only under the most extreme circumstances. Instead, it is a discipline to be practiced daily, habitually, even or especially in small matters, which are the training ground of character (Luke 16:10).

First John 4:19 puts the matter succinctly: "We love because he first loved us." Note that we are equipped to love others by first being loved ourselves. This leads to a crucial distinction. *It is only in a specific and limited sense that the New Testament authors ask us to deny ourselves.* They do not teach self-abnegation, that is, the loss or destruction of self. Christianity is not masochistic, and

---

4. The quotation is from Ps 69:9.

it should not promote, much less require, self-loathing. We are asked to give out of the abundance we have received, and for every loss, there is a corresponding, even greater gain. It is essential to understand, however, that this is not necessarily a gain *in kind*. There is no guarantee that finding our identity in God is going to make us famous or wealthy. Indeed, it is overwhelmingly likely to have the opposite effect.

The hard part is not doing what Jesus commands. The hard part is believing in the reality in which Jesus himself believed. If we do that, what he commands is perfectly sensible. What is impossible, and yet what most of us attempt most of the time, is to direct ourselves toward conventional goals while simultaneously trying to follow Jesus. We cannot serve God and worldly status any more than we can serve God and money. Indeed, a major part of what makes wealth so attractive is the status it and the things it buys convey. We do not need God to tell us we matter if our stuff already does the job.

It is worth emphasizing again that this is self-emptying of a particular sort. What follows "death on a cross" in Phil 2? Not destruction. "Therefore God also highly exalted him and gave him the name that is above every name." Jesus became nothing in this world, but he did not thereby become nothing. Indeed, the result was quite the opposite, but it took an act of immense faith and courage for him to take the downward step into God's exaltation. Jesus was tempted in the wilderness and then again in the garden to find an easier way, as we all are tempted to hedge our bets and locate our identity in something immediately tangible and self-evidently gratifying. The perspective of Heb 12:1–3 is similar:

> Therefore, since we are surrounded by so great a cloud of witnesses, let us also lay aside every weight and the sin that clings so closely, and let us run with perseverance the race that is set before us, looking to Jesus the pioneer and perfecter of our faith, who for the sake of the joy that was set before him endured the cross, disregarding its shame, and has taken his seat at the right hand of the throne of God. Consider him who en-

dured such hostility against himself from sinners, so that you may not grow weary or lose heart.

Once again, Jesus is the example, the "pioneer and perfecter," who disregarded human shame, endured the cross, and was ultimately exalted to the highest place of honor. Jesus was able to do this, not because he abandoned meaning, but "for the sake of the joy set before him." Loss in one reality meant gain in another. Likewise, "the joy set before us" ought to encourage us to lay aside those encumbrances that make us less effective disciples, even if that results in hostility from others. In short, self-denial is not the denial of self. It is trading meaning in one reality for meaning in another.

A final illustration is 1 Pet 2:21–23. Jesus was able to endure the world's abuse because he did not subject himself to the world's judgment.

> For to this you have been called, because Christ also suffered for you, leaving you an example, so that you should follow in his steps. "He committed no sin, and no deceit was found in his mouth." When he was abused, he did not return abuse; when he suffered, he did not threaten; but he entrusted himself to the one who judges justly.

Instead, "he entrusted himself" to God. To return to a phrase from the previous chapter, God the Father was Jesus's "significant other," the one whose opinion of him he believed.

Jesus knew who he was, and thus he was free to serve.

The Pattern of Jesus

Has anyone but Jesus lived with such utter disregard for social status?

The pattern is established even before his birth. Both Matthew and Luke report that Mary, although a virgin, became pregnant during the time of her engagement to Joseph. This was hardly an auspicious beginning, nor was Jesus's humble birth at the margins in Bethlehem. He grew up, not in the center of Jewish culture in Judea, but on its periphery, in "Galilee of the Gentiles" (Matt 4:15), in an insignificant town about which Nathanael later quipped, "Can anything good come out of Nazareth?" (John 1:46).

The Synoptic Gospels mention that Jesus was tempted in the wilderness prior to his ministry.[5] Matthew and Luke provide the more detailed account, in which Jesus is repeatedly given the opportunity to establish himself as the long-anticipated messiah.[6] The suggestion that he turn stones into bread (Matt 4:3–7) is a temptation to recreate the miracle of the manna in the wilderness under Moses, thus giving substance to contemporary messianic expectation. The second temptation is to make a miraculous demonstration at the site of the temple, the physical center of Judaism—again, tangibly proving that he fulfills his role. The third temptation is similar:

> Again, the devil took him to a very high mountain and showed him all the kingdoms of the world and their splendor; and he said to him, "All these I will give you, if you will fall down and worship me." (Matt 4:8–9)

Not coincidentally, the *final* scene in Matthew's Gospel occurs on a mountaintop. It is there that Jesus declares, "All authority in heaven and on earth has been given to me" (28:18). What the devil offers him twenty-four chapters earlier is a short cut. In effect, Jesus can assume all of the power and glory presently enjoyed by the Roman emperor without any cost to himself—that is, assuming that he is willing to do it the devil's way. This, of course, he refuses to do, and so his ministry—and his journey to the cross—begins.

Most of that ministry was conducted back in Galilee, where he made a habit of associating with common folk and reaching

---

5. Matthew, Mark, and Luke have many common elements and thus are referred to as "Synoptic," which means "viewed together."

6. Feldmeier provides a helpful analysis of the temptation stories in *Power, Service, Humility*, 1–9.

out to the lowly and despised, including tax collectors, prostitutes, and lepers, a tendency which did not go unnoticed by his social superiors. When presented with opportunities to impress leaders, Jesus nearly always used the occasion instead to challenge them (e.g., Luke 7:36–50; Mark 10:2–9; John 8:3–11). His handpicked disciples were themselves an undistinguished lot (Mark 1:16–20). In short, Jesus cultivated relationships with those who could do him the least good and undermined relationships with those whose assistance might best advance him.

Crowds began to follow Jesus, but he seemed bent on disappointing them. According to John 6:15, as a result of the feeding of the multitude, "Jesus realized that they were about to come and take him by force to make him king, [so] he withdrew again to the mountain by himself." We might say that the crowd succumbed to the temptation that Jesus himself had overcome, interpreting a feeding in the wilderness as a sign that Jesus would be the long-desired king. Later in that same chapter (John 6:48–66), Jesus's speech became so challenging and offensive that "many of his disciples turned back and no longer went about with him" (John 6:66). He was decidedly not in the business of winning friends and influencing people, at least not the sort of people whose accolades most of us cherish.

At one point, John the Baptist himself began to wonder why Jesus was not behaving in a more self-evidently messiah-like manner. From prison, he sent followers to question Jesus about his role. Matthew 11:4–6:

> Jesus answered them, "Go and tell John what you hear and see: the blind receive their sight, the lame walk, the lepers are cleansed, the deaf hear, the dead are raised, and the poor have good news brought to them. And blessed is anyone who takes no offense at me."

Taking offense at Jesus appears to have been the default human response.

Job applicants are known by their references. Note in Matt 11 those whom Jesus cited as his own are the blind, the lame, lepers, the deaf, the dead, and the poor. Indeed, God's favor toward the humble and the marginalized is a persistent theme in the Gospels. The same sentiment is found in Jesus's most famous teaching, the Beatitudes.[7] Matthew 5:3–5:

> Blessed are the poor in spirit, for theirs is the kingdom of heaven. Blessed are those who mourn, for they will be comforted. Blessed are the meek, for they will inherit the earth. Blessed are those who hunger and thirst for righteousness, for they will be filled.

We shall focus specifically on Jesus's teaching in the next chapter. For now, it is enough to observe that Jesus's words are in concert with his actions. What he said, he did.

When Jesus went up to the seat of power in Jerusalem for the last time, he made a public demonstration (Mark 11:1–10 and parallels) in fulfillment of the prophecy of Zech 9:9:

> Rejoice greatly, O daughter Zion! Shout aloud, O daughter Jerusalem! Lo, your king comes to you; triumphant and victorious is he, humble and riding on a donkey, on a colt, the foal of a donkey.

The irony is surely intentional. He is a king, yes, but the sort of king who enters Jerusalem on a donkey, accompanied not by an army but by a motley retinue of common folk.

In the city, he is again presented with multiple opportunities to prove himself to both religious (e.g., Mark 11:27–33 and 12:13–17) and civil (e.g., Mark 15:2–5 and Luke 23:6–16) authorities, which he repeatedly declines to do. Arrested in the night, he is then cruelly abused by Roman soldiers (Mark 15:16–20), who mock what they regard as his royal pretentions, most conspicuously by anointing him with a crown of thorns. He is then stripped and crucified between two criminals. In his agony, he is jeered at by observers and

---

7. There are two versions, in Matt 5:1–12 and Luke 6:20–31, which differ in significant ways.

abandoned by friends. Finally, he is hastily buried in a borrowed tomb.

One has to wonder, "How did he do it?" This is not simply an abstract theological question. If we are to follow Jesus, to emulate him especially in our character, we need to understand what made it possible for him to live as he did. How was his perspective different from ours? We cannot know enough from this distance to respond fully, but we can find a partial answer in Jesus's teaching, the subject to which we now turn.

CHAPTER FOUR

The Teaching of Jesus

Who among us is not concerned with winning and maintaining the good opinion of others? It is one of the most basic human motives, influencing our actions in ways both evident and unknown. At the same time, we are reluctant to admit the degree to which this aim governs our behavior. What candidate ever answered the question "Why do you want to be elected?" by saying, "I need to prove those jerks in high school wrong," or "I want to win my dad's approval"? What would we think of her if she did?

The clergy are little different from anyone else in this respect. Some pastoral appointments offer more visibility and prestige than others, and it is hard not to covet them at least partly for that reason, although we may tell ourselves that we are compelled only by the desire for greater service. The size of one's congregation is a ready point of comparison and thus serves as the default status gauge at clergy gatherings. Certain seminaries are more esteemed than others, and denominational affiliation itself carries status implications.

I referred at the beginning of the first chapter to the film *The African Queen*. One character I failed to mention is Rose Sayer's brother, Samuel, played by the British actor Robert Morley. Although serving as a missionary in Africa, Rev. Sayer's attention was focused on the career advancements of his fellow—and, in his mind, less deserving—colleagues back in England. His current ministry was thus seen almost as a punishment, and certainly not a service in which he could invest himself unreservedly. He is therefore a tragic figure, someone who cannot recognize and thereby free himself from the trap laid by his own ambition.

One of the most convicting passages of Scripture for those in professional ministry is surely Matt 23:5–7, which I paraphrase only slightly:

> They do all their deeds to be seen by others; for they make their robes long and put stripes on their sleeves. They love to have the place of honor at banquets and the best seats at sporting events, and to be greeted with respect at the mall, and to have people call them Reverend.

Churches themselves can be snobbish. Some will not hire a senior pastor who does not have the right accent or who does not possess a doctorate of some—really, almost any—sort. Christian subcultures have their own star systems, and, as in Hollywood and Nashville, proximity to fame is the convertible currency of status. The Corinthians might have been among the first Christian name droppers ("I belong to Paul. I belong to Apollos. I belong Cephas" [see 1 Cor 1:12]), but they were hardly the last. In short, in almost every way in which the church might have aped the world's status structures, it has.

Then there was Jesus. What made Jesus so different, and is it possible for us to share, if incompletely, in that difference? At least part of the answer lies in the response to another question, namely, what was the central theme of Jesus's teaching? The answer is simple but also somewhat mysterious. By far, the dominant subject of Jesus's instruction was the kingdom of God.[1]

---

1. Matthew's gospel uses the phrase "the kingdom of Heaven (lit. Heavens)" as a circumlocution, that is, a way of speaking of God without using the word "God." It does not refer only or specifically to a place called "Heaven(s)."

The "Kingdom" of God

The word "kingdom" (*basileia* in the original Greek) does not in this instance refer to a piece of land or a nation-state (e.g., the United Kingdom). The idea that Jesus was chiefly a political revolutionary reappears every few years in popular books, but it has been rejected roundly and consistently by biblical scholars. Too much evidence is stacked against it. Yes, one of Jesus's disciples, Simon, might have been a Zealot (Luke 6:15), but another, Matthew, was the polar opposite, a tax collector. Jesus himself commended a Roman centurion and healed his servant (Matt 8:5–10), and he taught his followers to "go the extra mile" if someone—that is, just such a soldier—compelled them to carry his load (Matt 5:41). Among other things, he also taught them to love their enemies (Luke 6:27), to pray for those who persecute them (Matt 5:44), to pay taxes to Caesar (Mark 12:13–17), and to put away the sword (Matt 26:52). Indeed, it was his very failure to act as a political figure that likely encouraged many to turn against him (Mark 15:6–11). Of course, Jesus's teaching about God's sovereignty had (and still has) profound political implications, but that he did not choose to employ political or military power must have baffled his contemporaries, friends and foes alike.

If not a territory or a state, what is the kingdom of God? Hebrew Scripture speaks of God as "king" in numerous Psalms (5:2; 10:6; 24:7–8; 29:10; 44:4, etc.), and in a range of other books, such as Numbers (23:21), 1 Samuel (8:7), Isaiah (43:15), and Malachi (1:14). It is an understandable designation given the fact that the king (the precise title varied) was the most powerful figure and the preeminent judge in most contemporary cultures. That God's kingship had to be asserted is noteworthy. The kingdom of God was something acknowledged by faith, sometimes in the face of the enemy's derision ("Where is your God?" [cf. Ps 79:10; Joel 2:17; Mic 7:10]) or the believer's own disappointment.

In the New Testament, the phrase may be helpfully translated as "the reign of God,"[2] which is exercised where and to the extent

---

2. The "dominion of God" and "rule of God" are also suitable translations.

that God's purposes are realized. Consider the second verse of the Lord's Prayer: "Your kingdom come. Your will be done, on earth as it is in heaven" (Matt 6:10). In the coming reign of God, the will of God shall be as fully obeyed on earth as it is now in heaven. It follows that the reign of God is at least partially present wherever God's will is done today.

This explains what would otherwise be a fundamental contradiction in the evidence: Jesus spoke of the kingdom or reign of God as something manifest in his own ministry but also as a future, perhaps distantly future, reality. This is one of many instances in theology in which the "both/and" answer is a great deal more convincing than the "either/or."

God's Present Reign

Numerous texts evidence the fact that Jesus regarded God's reign as "breaking in" or specially present in his own ministry. The Synoptic Gospels provide two different accounts of the launch of Jesus's public ministry, but in both cases the foundational message is much the same.[3] According to Mark:

> Now after John was arrested, Jesus came to Galilee, proclaiming the good news of God, "The time is fulfilled, and *the kingdom of God has come near;* repent, and believe in the good news." (1:14–15)

British scholar C. H. Dodd famously argued that the Greek verb *ēngiken* should be translated "has arrived,"[4] but most interpreters have concluded that a translation such as that quoted above ("has come near" in the NRSV) is more accurate. The reign of God is now dawning and in that sense is present, but it has not yet fully ar-

---

3. As noted in the previous chapter, Matthew, Mark, and Luke are referred to as the Synoptics, which means "viewed together," because of their many similarities.

4. C. H. Dodd, *The Parables of the Kingdom* (Glasgow: Collins, 1961), 36–37.

rived. The substance of this verse is paralleled in other texts in the New Testament that are thought to contain baptismal formulae, such as Rom 3:12, and therefore appears to represent a common perspective:

Mark 1:15	Romans 13:12
The time has been fulfilled	The night is far gone
The dominion of God has come near	The day has drawn near
Repent	Let us put off the works of darkness
Believe in the good news	Let us wake up and be sober.[5]

Unlike Mark and Matthew, Luke used Jesus's words in the synagogue at Nazareth as his inaugural. Jesus unrolled the scroll of Isaiah and read to the congregation:

"The Spirit of the Lord is upon me, because he has anointed me to bring good news to the poor. He has sent me to proclaim release to the captives and recovery of sight to the blind, to let the oppressed go free, to proclaim the year of the Lord's favor." (Luke 4:18–19)

The quoted text is from the latter chapters of Isaiah (61:1–2),[6] a portion of the Old Testament prophetic writings that focuses on the hoped for restoration of the people of Israel following the Babylonian Exile. The chief entity in several of these chapters is the "Servant of the Lord," a figure with whom Jesus himself appears to have identified.[7] That the anticipated restoration had not yet come in all its fullness would have been obvious to Jesus's hearers, and no one present would have been surprised by the text itself. It was what happened immediately after that caught them off guard:

5. 1. Adapted from Joel Marcus, *Mark 1–8: A New Introduction and Commentary*, AB 27 (New York: Doubleday, 2000), 174. I strongly encourage serious Bible students to secure a copy of this insightful commentary. It is a joy to read.

6. See also Isa 58:6.

7. On the use of "servant" language throughout the Bible, see Don N. Howell, Jr., *Servants of the Servant: A Biblical Theology of Leadership* (Eugene, OR: Wipf & Stock, 2003).

And Jesus rolled up the scroll, gave it back to the attendant, and sat down. The eyes of all in the synagogue were fixed on him. Then he began to say to them, "Today this scripture has been fulfilled in your hearing." (Luke 4:20–21)

Jesus claimed the prophetic anointing for himself and announced that the long-anticipated time of restoration, "the year of the Lord's favor," was upon them. According to the Gospels, this was too much for his hometown audience to swallow. "And they took offense at him" (Mark 6:3b).

Another example is Jesus's statement about the binding of the strong man in Mark 3:27 and its parallels. Jesus's enemies had accused him of casting out demons "by the ruler of the demons" (3:22). He responded by arguing that it made no sense for demons to cast out demons, that "a house divided against itself . . . will not stand" (3:25). Moreover, "No one can enter a strong man's house and plunder his property without first tying up the strong man; then indeed the house can be plundered" (3:27). The background to this exchange is the apocalyptic belief that the present world is in the thrall of Satan. To say that Satan is now bound is to assert that a fundamental power shift had already occurred.

An especially prominent saying about the presence of God's reign in the ministry of Jesus is found in Luke 17:20–21. A group of Pharisees pressed Jesus for specific details about the future. Jesus answered,

"The kingdom of God is not coming with things that can be observed; nor will they say, 'Look, here it is! or 'There it is!' For, in fact, the kingdom of God is among you."

Jesus did not wholly contradict his opponents' future expectation, although he did challenge the popular notion that its arrival could be foreseen through observance of visible signs. The larger problem was that his questioners could not see that God's reign was already active in their midst. It is noteworthy that this account immediately follows the story of the healing of the ten lepers. It was the foreigner, a Samaritan leper, who saw what the insiders missed. He alone praised God and returned to thank Jesus.

That religious insiders could not recognize God's initiative is, in a way, understandable. One is conservative to the extent that one has something to conserve. (In that sense, everyone is conservative about something.) Religious leaders preserve and hand down a faith tradition, an important and natively conservative function. A special sensitivity is required to adapt—not merely to transmit or, at the opposite end, to abrogate—tradition. It is an inherently risky and inevitably controversial role. That Jesus should have been at odds with religious leaders is therefore unsurprising.[8]

Some have preferred to translate the final phrase in Luke 17:21 as "the kingdom of God is *within* you." This correlates with the contemporary emphasis on personal spirituality (as in, "I am spiritual, not religious"), so it is hardly surprising that interpreters occasionally champion this reading. Nevertheless, the idea that Jesus saw God's reign as something wholly "spiritual" (e.g., as God's rule over the hearts of believers) is unfounded. Instead, the evidence of the Gospels confirms that Jesus anticipated a future in which God's rule would extend over the whole material cosmos. Importantly, the present-day harbingers of that future were mostly physical acts, such as the blind receiving their sight and lepers being healed (Matt 11:4). That there is an individual and internal component to God's reign can hardly be doubted, but that is not by any means the whole story.

8. So many controversies within our own churches boil down to this: one group attempts to hold onto something deemed precious, while another attempts to accommodate it to some new reality. The baby-with-the-bathwater idiom is often employed in such situations, but it is a deceptive analogy: where baby ends and bathwater begins is obvious enough, but the line between faithful and unfaithful stewardship of the tradition is seldom so clear. It is tragic that Christians so often fail to acknowledge, much less to respect, the integrity of other believers with whom they disagree. Of course, the same could be said for humans generally.

God's Future Reign

Based on these and a handful of other texts,[9] it is evident that Jesus thought that God's long-awaited reign was already active in his ministry. A significantly greater body of evidence, however, demonstrates that Jesus also believed in a future arrival of God's dominion in all its fullness. We earlier cited the first petition of the Lord's Prayer: "Your kingdom come" (Matt 6:10). To that could be added a great many other references, such as the Beatitudes (Matt 5:3–12 and Luke 6:20–23), which vividly contrast the present and the future state of the righteous. For example, "Blessed are the meek, for they *will* inherit the earth" (Matt 5:5). Many of Jesus's parables anticipate a future judgment and righting of wrongs, such as in The Sheep and the Goats, The Rich Fool, The Banquet, The Net, The Wheat and the Weeds, and The Wicked Tenants.[10] A few parables specifically depict God's reign as being already present but yet largely hidden, awaiting full manifestation (e.g., The Growing Seed, The Leaven, and The Mustard Seed).[11]

Jesus's future expectation is front and center in passages such as Mark 13:1–4, the prediction of the Jerusalem temple's destruction (also in 15:29 and alluded to in John 2:19), and in the apocalyptic warnings found in the remainder of Mark 13.[12] The most notable prediction concerns the coming of The Son of Man (Mark 13:24–27), which echoes the influential prophecy of Dan 7:13. Some argue that these Gospel texts tell us more about the beliefs of the first-century church than those of Jesus himself. There is no simple or certain way of making such a determination since what we know of Jesus does indeed come to us via his followers. On the other hand, it is overwhelmingly likely that the early church's hopes were in basic continuity with those of Jesus

9. For example, see Mark 2:18–20 and Luke 11:20.

10. Luke 12:13–21; Matt 22:1–10//Luke 14:15–24; Matt 13:47–50; Matt 13:24–30, 36–43; and Mark 12:1–12//Matt 21:33–46//Luke 20:9–19.

11. Mark 4:26; Matt 13:33//Luke 13:20–21; and Mark 4:30//Matt 13:31–32//Luke 13:18–20.

12. Compare the parallel passages in Matt 24 and Luke 21.

himself.[13] That is not to say that there was no development of ideas or shift in emphasis over time, especially due to the fact that the church lived in a post-Easter context. Still, it is a very great stretch to posit an essential discontinuity between Jesus and his followers on so central an issue, especially in view of the quantity of contrary evidence at every level of the tradition. Jesus is the middle term between Judaism, on the one side, and Christianity, on the other. A plausible historical Jesus must be both sufficiently the product of Judaism and adequately the cause of Christianity. The eschatological orientation of Jesus in the Gospels fits the bill perfectly.

Finally, we should note that Jesus did not regard his impending death as the conclusion, much less the defeat, of his mission. Had he done so, he could have taken steps to avoid this fate. The Lord's Supper is one of the best attested traditions about Jesus, being found in all of the Synoptic Gospels and, just as significantly, in 1 Cor 11:23–26, probably the earliest written account.[14] Each version of the story includes the expectation of Jesus's future vindication. For example, in Mark 14:25 Jesus says, "Truly I tell you, I will never again drink of the fruit of the vine until that day when I drink it new in the kingdom of God." Paul adds this comment to the words of institution: "For as often as you eat this bread and drink the cup, you proclaim the Lord's death until he comes" (1 Cor 11:26). Such an expectation is consistent with the portrayal of the ultimate vindication of the Suffering Servant in Isa 40-55, the righteous person in the Psalms (e.g., Ps 34:19), and the just martyr in intertestamental Jewish literature.[15]

We noted in the previous chapter that it is sensible to follow

---

13. I argue this case in some detail in *In God's Time: The Bible and the Future* (Grand Rapids: Eerdmans, 2002), 130–42.

14. Mark 14:22–25; Matt 26:26–29; Luke 22:15–20. The author of John's Gospel also appears to have known some version of the Lord's Supper tradition. See John 6:48–55 and 13:1–30.

15. See, for example, the story of the martyrdom of the seven brothers and their mother in 2 Macc 7. The second bother tells the evil king, "'You accursed wretch, you dismiss us from this present life, but the King of the universe will raise us up to an everlasting renewal of life, because we have died for his laws'" (v. 9).

Jesus to the extent that one believes what Jesus himself believed. Among the most central of such beliefs is the conviction that God's reign is both a present and a future reality. One might even say that for Jesus, God's reign is *the* true reality. To isolate Jesus's ethic from this belief is inevitably to diminish and misrepresent it. Jesus's beliefs about God's reign make sense of his mindset and his teaching, both of which turned conventional thinking about status upside down.

Reversal in God's "Kingdom"

Two themes in Jesus's teaching about God's reign are worth highlighting for the purpose of this study: reversal in and the value of God's reign. We have already mentioned the Beatitudes, which compare the humble present and the exalted future state of the righteous.[16] Luke's version also includes a series of woes in which the fortunes of the prosperous are reversed:

> But woe to you who are rich, for you have received your
>   consolation.
> Woe to you who are full now, for you will be hungry.
> Woe to you who are laughing now, for you will mourn and
>   weep.
> Woe to you when all speak well of you, for that is what their
>   ancestors did to the false prophets. (Luke 6:24–26)

This passage echoes Mary's song of praise, the Magnificat, found earlier in Luke:

> He has looked with favor on the lowliness of his servant. . . . He
> has scattered the proud in the thoughts of their hearts. He has

---

16. Examples of such reversal in the Old Testament include the Song of Hannah (1 Sam 2:1–10), echoed in the Magnificat (quoted above); Ps 112:5–8, 149:4; and Prov 3:34, 11:2, 15:33, 18:12, and 22:4. On "Reversal as Jewish motif," see Matthew R. Malcolm, *Paul and the Rhetoric of Reversal in 1 Corinthians: The Impact of Paul's Gospel on His Macro-Rhetoric* (Cambridge: Cambridge University Press, 2013), 7–26.

brought down the powerful from their thrones, and lifted up the lowly; he has filled the hungry with good things, and sent the rich away empty. (2:48a, 51b–53)

This theme of eschatological (or final) reversal is common in the Gospels, best summarized by Mark 10:31: "Many who are first will be last, and the last will be first." It is taught in parables such as The Workers in the Vineyard, The Wicked Tenants, The Banquet, and The Rich Fool.[17] Similarly, a collection of Jesus's sayings turns on the distinction between earthly and heavenly, present and (primarily) future rewards. Not coincidentally, the attitude most frequently challenged is the desire for worldly recognition. For example, in Matthew we find:

Beware of practicing your piety before others in order to be seen by them; for then you have no reward from your Father in heaven. So whenever you give alms, do not sound a trumpet before you, as the hypocrites do in the synagogues and in the streets, so that they may be praised by others. Truly I tell you, they have received their reward. (6:1–2)

And whenever you pray, do not be like the hypocrites; for they love to stand and pray in the synagogues and at the street corners, so that they may be seen by others. Truly I tell you, they have received their reward. But whenever you pray, go into your room and shut the door and pray to your Father who is in secret; and your Father who sees in secret will reward you. (6:5–6)

And whenever you fast, do not look dismal, like the hypocrites, for they disfigure their faces so as to show others that they are fasting. Truly I tell you, they have received their reward. But when you fast, put oil on your head and wash your face, so that your fasting may be seen not by others but by your Father who is in secret; and your Father who sees in secret will reward you. (6:16–18)

17. Matt 20:1–6; Mark 12:1–12; Matt 22:1–14; and Luke 12:13–21.

Then as now, Jesus's teaching is in sharp contrast to the human tendency to seek a commensurate public return on private acts of goodness. As Dio Chrysostom observed, "For all men set great store by the outward tokens of high achievement, and not one man in a thousand is willing to agree that what he regards as a noble deed shall have been done for himself alone and that no other man shall have knowledge of it."[18]

Note that Jesus did not ask his hearers to become nothing. It is the source of their significance, not their need for significance, that was challenged. Characteristically, Jesus required them to set aside one thing because it stood in the way of their receiving something better. Jesus's teaching about wealth follows the same logic:

> When you give a luncheon or a dinner, do not invite your friends or your brothers or your relatives or rich neighbors, in case they may invite you in return, and you would be repaid. But when you give a banquet, invite the poor, the crippled, the lame, and the blind. And you will be blessed, because they cannot repay you, for you will be repaid at the resurrection of the righteous. (Luke 14:12b–14)

Perhaps most uncomfortable for us in the West is this instruction in Matthew:

> Do not store up for yourselves treasures on earth, where moth and rust consume and where thieves break in and steal; but store up for yourselves treasures in heaven, where neither moth nor rust consumes and where thieves do not break in and steal. For where your treasure is, there your heart will be also. (Matt 6:19–20)

---

18. Dio Chrysostom, *Rhod.* (*Or.* 31) 22 (Cohoon and Crosby, LCL). Compare Pliny the Younger's assessment of human nature: "Very few people are as scrupulously honest in secret as in public, and many are influenced by public opinion but scarcely anyone by conscience" (Pliny the Younger, *Ep.* 3.20.8–9 [Radice, LCL]).

The parable of The Sower makes a similar point: "And others are those sown among the thorns: these are the ones who hear the word, but the cares of the world, and the lure of wealth, and the desire for other things come in and choke the word, and it yields nothing" (Matt 4:18–19). Perhaps the best known saying of all on the subject is Matt 6:24b: "You cannot serve God and wealth." The addition to the story in Luke's account is striking. Jesus's statement was ridiculed by a group of religious leaders, to whom he responded, "You are those who justify yourselves in the sight of others" (Luke 16:15a).

That is a sobering statement. Material prosperity, together with the security and status it affords, is far too easily assumed to be a sign of God's favor. That spiritual blessedness and wealth are inextricably intertwined is the core assertion of the so-called prosperity gospel, according to whose teachers "Everyone possessed the God-given potential to sow and reap their financial harvest with plenty to spare. Poverty marked a spiritual shortage."[19] By this reasoning, ostentatious displays of affluence, such as a megachurch pastor's 1.7 million dollar house, are not only permitted but actively encouraged.[20] Such extremes are indeed outrageous, but they are also too safe a target. We are all tempted to cover our naked ambitions with a blanket of sanctity.

The Supreme Value of God's Reign

Adapting the concept of the significant other, we could say that our god is the person or thing that tells us who we are. We serve money and material possessions when we allow ourselves to be defined by them, when we look to them to justify us. "Do you know who I am? Just look at my car, my clothes, my 401(k)." Jesus himself was as unconcerned with material possessions as he was with

19. Kate Bowler, *Blessed: A History of the American Prosperity Gospel* (New York: Oxford University Press, 2013), 95.

20. Carol Kuruvilla, "Pastor Calls Swanky $1.7 Million Mansion a 'Gift from God,'" *New York Daily News,* October 30, 2013.

social status. That is hardly surprising since the two are nearly always conjoined.

Given all that we have seen, we would expect Jesus to value humility in his followers, as in fact he did.[21] It was the poor and seemingly inconsequential widow whose gift was most prized (Mark 12:41–44). It was the penitent tax collector, not the self-righteous Pharisee, who was honored (Luke 18:10–14). Jesus praised God for having revealed "these things" to the lowly, "for such was your gracious will" (Matt 11:25–26), and he commended the faith of children (Matt 19:13–15). More than once, he is reported to have said, "All who exalt themselves will be humbled, and those who humble themselves will be exalted" (e.g., Luke 14:11; 18:14; and Matt 23:12).

Jesus believed that one's worldly status was both temporary and, in a sense, illusory. What matters is what is true ultimately, and it is clear that Jesus considered God's reign to be the true and final reality. But, as we saw in the previous chapter, this was not simply a future verity for Jesus. He showed no concern for his own standing, spending most of his days in the company of the socially insignificant and marginalized. He taught by his actions that God's love extends beyond the boundaries of propriety. He touched lepers, ate with tax collectors, forgave sinners, and showed favor to Samaritans and Romans. Once again, parables conveyed the message. For example, The Lost Coin, The Lost Sheep and Prodigal Son tell of God's extravagant outreach to sinners. In The Good Samaritan and The Pharisee and the Tax Collector, it is the outsider, not the professionally religious, who models true faith.

The second theme mentioned above, the supreme value of God's reign, was also conveyed in parables:

> The kingdom of heaven is like treasure hidden in a field, which someone found and hid; then in his joy he goes and sells all that he has and buys that field. Again, the kingdom of heaven

---

21. A fine overview of the concept of humility in the New Testament writings is provided by Feldmeier, *Power, Service, Humility*, 61–93. I refer to this insightful work several times in the pages that follow.

is like a merchant in search of fine pearls; on finding one pearl of great value, he went and sold all that he had and bought it (Matt 13:44–46)

The figure in both parables is joyous at the discovery, not resentful at its cost. Indeed, the cost seems a comparative trifle in view of the anticipated gain. As we have seen, this is in perfect harmony with other of Jesus's teachings. It is also reminiscent of Paul's account of his costly discipleship in Philippians:

> More than that, I regard everything as loss because of the surpassing value of knowing Christ Jesus my Lord. For his sake I have suffered the loss of all things, and I regard them as rubbish, in order that I may gain Christ. (Phil 3:8)

Of course, the sincerity of one's convictions is proved by one's life, not by one's words. Jesus's belief in the surpassing value of God's reign was best demonstrated by all that he abandoned for its sake. Unlike us, Jesus did not hedge his bets. He walked an increasingly lonely path in which authorities opposed him, popular opinion turned against him, and close associates denied and betrayed him. It is easy to believe in God's reign as an exalted concept that costs us little. It was no mere proposition to Jesus.

The Glory of Jesus in the Gospel of John

As we would anticipate, John's Gospel offers a distinctive but complementary perspective. Of particular interest for this study is its employment of the term "glory."[22] The word is used numerous times in the Gospels, especially with reference to the majesty of

---

22. The Greek word *doxa* comes from the verb *dokein*, meaning "to seem." In non-biblical Greek, the word usually means "opinion," as in the English "orthodoxy" (right + opinion). In biblical use, including the Septuagint, it most often means "glory," "majesty" or "radiance," as in the English "doxology" (glory + saying).

God and of the coming Son of Man,[23] but it has a distinctive edge and prominence in John. In a number of cases, it is close in meaning to "praise," "honor" and "approval." In John 5:44, Jesus says, "How can you believe when you accept glory from one another and do not seek the glory that comes from the one who alone is God?" This contrast between human and divine recognition is a leitmotif of John. So, for example:

> Those who speak on their own seek their own glory; but the one who seeks the glory of him who sent him is true, and there is nothing false in him. (John 7:18)

And again:

> Nevertheless many, even of the authorities, believed in him. But because of the Pharisees they did not confess it, for fear that they would be put out of the synagogue; for they loved human glory more than the glory that comes from God. (John 12:42–43)

Jesus is the one who receives and shares "the glory that comes from God"—glory that was his even "before the world existed" (John 17:5, 22; see 1:1–5). Jesus himself does "not accept glory from human beings" (John 5:41). Indeed, he does not pursue his own glory, but that of the Father (John 7:18). Likewise, it is the Father's will to glorify the Son: "I do not seek my own glory; there is one who seeks it and he is the judge" (John 8:50).

In a programmatic verse—John 1:14—the evangelist writes, "And the Word became flesh and lived among us, and we have seen his glory [majesty], the glory as of a father's only son, full of grace and truth." The careful reader is reminded of Ex 33:18–19, in which Moses petitions God, "Show me your glory, I pray." God answers,

> I will make all my goodness pass before you, and will proclaim before you the name, "The Lord"; and I will be gracious to

23. For example, Matt 16:27; Mark 8:38; and Luke 2:9.

whom I will be gracious, and will show mercy on whom I will show mercy.

It is this glory that is revealed, that "passes before them," in Jesus's gracious words and works (John 2:11; 11:4; 17:4) and, especially, in his sacrificial death, "the hour" of his glorification (John 12:23–24; 13:31–32; 17:1–4). Following his resurrection, Jesus returned to glory "in the Father's presence" (John 17:5). It was only at that point that his closest followers comprehended what had transpired in their midst: "His disciples did not understand these things at first; but when Jesus was glorified, then they remembered that these things had been written of him and had been done to him" (John 12:16). This was in keeping with Jesus's promise that the Spirit would remind them of what Jesus said (John 14:26) and so glorify him (John 16:14).

Jesus's followers themselves may also glorify God through their actions: "My Father is glorified by this, that you bear much fruit and become my disciples" (John 15:8), and Jesus promised to bestow glory on the faithful (John 12:26; 17:22). It is likely that this Gospel was written to a Jewish-Christian community that had become estranged from the synagogue following the destruction of Jerusalem in 70 CE. Clearly, it assumes that hostility toward believers is now the norm:

> If the world hates you, be aware that it hated me before it hated you. If you belonged to the world, the world would love you as its own. Because you do not belong to the world, but I have chosen you out of the world—therefore the world hates you. (John 15:18–19)

It stands to reason that for John, the honor bestowed by the world on "its own" and the honor bestowed by God on the faithful are mutually exclusive. This observation helps to explain why glory occupies so central a place in this Gospel. The moment at which opposition to Jesus crystallized—his crucifixion—was the occasion at which God's majestic character, God's glory, was fully revealed. Thus, the cross does not prove that God rejected Jesus, as opponents might claim. On the contrary, for those with eyes to see, it is the truest evidence of Jesus's identity with God, who is Love.

All of this talk of glory might well seem foreign and even off-putting to modern readers. Moreover, most of us do not live (or at least do not perceive ourselves as living) in a world of such stark choices. Religious texts composed in a climate of persecution and marginalization often see the world in highly polarized, black-or-white terms. Prominent among these are the biblical apocalypses, Daniel and Revelation. What I earlier wrote about their value could just as well be said for the Gospel of John:

> [They] take us into a world in which one's decision for God is immediately pressing and ultimately costly ... they challenge our measured alliance with God and our easy association with worldly power.... Few of us are forced to choose explicitly between worldly and divine approval, so few of us ever consider the matter seriously.... [they] challenge us to question our deepest motivations and attachments.[24]

A Remarkable Consistency

A remarkable consistency runs through Jesus's character, teachings, and life. He lived as one who wholly believed that God's reign was the ultimate reality and the enduring source of meaning. The early church? Not so much.

Perhaps we should take heart in knowing that the first generation of Christians was almost as fallible as we are. Had they been otherwise, the New Testament would contain much less instruction relevant to this book. Instead, its authors confronted the all-too-natural problems arising from human status seeking, such as jealousy, gossip, one-upmanship, slander and division. How the New Testament writers dealt with these problems is the subject of the next few chapters.

24. Hill, *In God's Time*, 128.

CHAPTER FIVE

Slow of Heart: The Disciples

Then Jesus said to them, "Oh, how foolish you are, and how slow of heart to believe all that the prophets have declared! Was it not necessary that the Messiah should suffer these things and then enter into his glory?"

(LUKE 24:25–26)

I have noticed an interesting phenomenon. Some students who struggle the most initially retain more of their learning over the long haul than others who are a quick study. It appears to be a case of "less easy come, less easy go." They were a bit slower to grasp the material and acquire the facts, but the lessons stuck, probably because these students had invested so much more in the effort.

In Luke 24:25, the resurrected Jesus describes the disciples as "slow of heart." That elegant phrase unmasks the disciples' problem. Their incomprehension during the ministry of Jesus was not due to stupidity. Instead, their fault was a wrong orientation. They came to Jesus with traditional expectations about his—and by extension, their—role. Moreover, their hopes were in sync with the conventional human desire for status and security. That convention had to be shattered before Jesus's followers could grasp what he was about. The disciples were slow, but when at last they learned the lesson, they took it to heart.

Religion as a Market Economy

Religion in the Greco-Roman world served a range of purposes. We might be inclined to disparage pagan religions as superstitious, secretive, exclusive, or even demonic. Such sweeping judgments do not do justice to the fact that countless persons made genuinely pious commitments and experienced genuinely religious feeling within the context of the beliefs and rituals they knew (Acts 17:22–31). Then as now, religion connected everyday people to the vast power, mystery, and purpose of the universe. It also served as the glue that held together communities. Granted, that glue could also bind persons to their place within a rigid hierarchy, but its effects on society were in many ways salutary. Of course, beliefs and practices varied widely, and I am not meaning to defend every religious act or idea, some of which were indeed oppressive and cruel. Still, for most people most of the time, religion was experienced as a positive element in a normal way of life.

The central ritual in most ancient religions was sacrifice, usually of a domesticated animal, but also of grains, fruits, and incense. The Roman philosopher Porphyry distinguished three main purposes: to honor the god(s), to express gratitude, and to petition for some good.[1] Any of these acts could be motivated by sincere piety, and any could be abused. Civic festivals often included sacrifices that were underwritten by a high-ranking sponsor. The crowds would join in eating the meat of the sacrificial animals, and their patron would receive public recognition. So, then as now, a well-to-do citizen could use religion as a means of social advancement. Public religion is less ubiquitous today; nevertheless, it remains prudent for an American politician with high aspirations to maintain at least a nominal association with a faith community.

It must have been easy to regard the third type of sacrifice, that which accompanies a prayer, as a quid-pro-quo transaction. Religion is always in danger of degenerating into a barter system. One seeks to make a deal with the cosmos, and religion names the price and mediates the sale. The ancient temple thus would

---

1. Porphyry, *Abst.* 2.24.

function rather like a super-sized vending machine. Insert, for example, a sheep (the cost of the animal corresponding to the size of the request), pull the lever (correct ritual performed by the right sort of priest), and out pop good crops, healing, long life, or an heir. We no longer engage in animal sacrifice, but the scenario is nonetheless familiar. Most of us have tried through similar manipulation to have our will done on earth by heaven. Of course, we are encouraged to "let our requests be made known to God" (Phil 4:6), but petitions are not purchases, and church is not Walmart.

Jews also made sacrifices to worship God and to express gratitude. Additionally, sacrifices were employed to cleanse from impurity and, most notably, to atone for sin. Sacrifice was also the occasion for prayer, as in the story of the dedication of Solomon's temple in 1 Kings 8. The very human temptation to regard sacrifice as a kind of magic or as a way of bribing God also existed within Judaism. Hence, Samuel's rebuke of Saul: "Has the Lord as great delight in burnt offerings and sacrifices, as in obedience to the voice of the Lord? Surely, to obey is better than sacrifice, and to heed than the fat of rams" (1 Sam 15:22; see Ps 40:6 and Hos 6:6). Sacrifice was the expression, not the substance, of piety.

Quid Pro Quo

The linkage between right behavior, "obedience to the voice of the Lord," and God's blessing is deeply ingrained in Judaism. At Sinai, God's promise to the Israelites is conditional: "*If* you obey my voice and keep my covenant, you shall be my treasured possession out of all the peoples" (Exod 19:5). The very next chapter provides the principal account of what is to be "obeyed and kept"—the Ten Commandments.

It is important to add that there always was more to Judaism than rules and rewards. In particular, God was known to be gracious, loving, and forgiving. According to Ps 103:10–12:

He does not deal with us according to our sins,
Nor repay us according to our iniquities.

> For as the heavens are high above the earth,
> so great is his steadfast love toward those who fear him;
> so far as the east is from the west,
> so far he removes our transgressions from us.

Yom Kippur, the annual day of atonement (Lev 16:29–31), tangibly demonstrated that God's relationship with Israel was based on something more than the people's performance. A covenant relationship is more than a legal contract.

Nevertheless, any religion with rules can be reduced to rule-keeping, a trap into which Christians as well as Jews sometimes fall. It is easy to see how a text such as Deut 28 might encourage mechanistic, this-for-that moral bookkeeping. Deuteronomy 28:1–14 relates the catalog of blessings to be showered upon obedient Israel, including abundant crops and progeny, success in battle, and even prominence amongst the nations:

> The Lord will make you the head, and not the tail; you shall be only at the top, and not at the bottom—if you obey the commandments of the Lord your God, which I am commanding you today, by diligently observing them. (28:13)

There is a flip side. Deuteronomy 28:15–68, the much longer portion of the chapter, lists the curses that will come upon the people if they disobey. These include disaster, panic, pestilence, drought, madness, and blindness.

Little wonder then that Jesus's disciples should ask, "Rabbi, who sinned, this man or his parents, that he was born blind?" (John 9:2). Jesus's reply challenges their presupposition: "'Neither this man nor his parents sinned; he was born blind so that God's works might be revealed in him'" (John 9:3). The assumed curse/blessing calculation was invalidated—as it would later be in the cross (Gal 3:13). In both instances, what seemed a place of cursing was in fact the very place God was powerfully present. Such is the divine economy, and such is the perspective that the Markan disciples—and a great many early Christians after them—struggled to comprehend.

After he had been healed by Jesus, the now-sighted man was questioned by a contentious panel of religious leaders. Exasperated by the man's answers, they closed the inquiry by appealing to their—patently obvious, it seemed—moral superiority: "You were born entirely in sins, and are you trying to teach us?" (John 9:34). Although wrongly founded, their presumption is comprehensible. Bad things are supposed to happen to bad people. That is also the perspective of Job's accusers:

> Think now, who that was innocent ever perished?
> Or where were the upright cut off?
> As I have seen, those who plow iniquity
> and sow trouble reap the same.
> By the breath of God they perish,
> and by the blast of his anger they are consumed. (Job 4:7–9)

All of this is said to provide context. In the ancient world broadly, it was customary to think that one's correct performance of religious duty, whether in the making of sacrifices or in the obeying of laws, would result in tangible, physical, worldly—and, one might hope, immediate—benefits, such as health, prosperity and, yes, status ("the head, and not the tail . . . at the top, and not at the bottom" [Deut 28:13]). Jesus did not see things that way, and it is understandable that those who followed him were sluggish learners. Being slow of heart ourselves, we can benefit from their example, seeing ourselves in their mistakes and emulating their eventual progress as Jesus's disciples.

Preliminary Considerations

Before venturing further, however, we need to clarify our terms. The word "disciple" translates the Greek *mathētēs*, which could also be rendered "student," "learner," "adherent," or "follower." (It is related to the verb *manthanein*, "to learn.") "Disciple" is used 261 times in the New Testament, mostly in the Gospels, and is employed in three distinct ways. Most broadly, it describes anyone who follows a teacher or movement, such as disciples of the Pharisees (Matt 22:15–16), disciples of Moses (John 9:24–29), and disciples of John the Baptist (Mark 2:18).[2] Secondly, it refers to all who identify with Jesus, including persons such as Joseph of Arimathea (Matt 27:57) and the anonymous man who asked Jesus to let him "go and bury my father" (Matt 8:21). Several women were counted among Jesus's followers, and one, Tabitha, is explicitly called a disciple (Acts 9:36).[3] In John 4:1, the Pharisees complain that "Jesus is making and baptizing more disciples than John" (see also John 6:60; 7:3; 13:35), and Matthew's Gospel concludes with the Great Commission, in which Jesus commanded his hearers to "Go . . . and make disciples of all nations" (28:19).

The third usage is the most familiar, and the one we shall assume throughout the remainder of this chapter: *the* disciples are Jesus's inner circle, those who followed him throughout most of his ministry. A number of passages refer specifically to "the twelve" disciples (e.g., Matt 11:1 and Mark 4:10), whom Jesus chose to be his companions and whom he often took aside and taught separately (e.g., Mark 3:34).[4] The most trenchant description is that found in Mark 3:14: the Twelve were those appointed "to be with him." (Now, there is a sermon in four words.) Theirs was an unusually demanding discipleship, requiring them to leave jobs and family and travel with Jesus. Unlike a rabbinic apprenticeship, it was an open-ended (and ultimately lifelong) commitment.

It is frequently unclear whether the phrase "the disciples" refers only to this group, to a somewhat larger cluster of Jesus's most dedicated followers, or to a still more generalized body of

2. The usual verb for describing the action of a disciple is *akolouthein,* "to follow."

3. Mark's Gospel, on which we shall focus below, provides "a consistently positive portrayal of Jesus's female followers," presenting them "as role models of faith (5:34), insight (7:29), prescient devotion (14:3–9), and faithfulness (15:40–41)." Larry W. Hurtado, "Following Jesus in the Gospel of Mark—and Beyond," in *Patterns of Discipleship in the New Testament,* ed. Richard N. Longenecker (Grand Rapids: Eerdmans, 1996), 24. This is in stark contrast to Mark's ambiguous treatment of the male disciples.

4. The significance of the number twelve will be discussed below.

adherents. It is reasonable to assume, however, that the Twelve are typically included whenever "the disciples" or "his disciples" are mentioned in the Gospels.

Adding to the confusion is the sometimes interchangeable use of the word "apostle." An apostle (from *apostellein*, "to send") is one sent forth, for example, as a missionary. The word is used to describe the Twelve in a handful of passages in the Gospels, such as Matt 10:2 ("These are the names of the twelve apostles") and Mark 6:30 ("The apostles," who had been sent out by Jesus, returned and "told him all that they had done and taught"). It is commonly employed this way in Acts, where, for example, Matthias is chosen to take Judas's place as the twelfth apostle (1:26). But the word is used elsewhere to refer to a wider group of early church leaders, including James, the brother of Jesus (Gal 1:19) and, of course, the apostle Paul (e.g., Acts 14:4 and Gal 1:1). Then there is Heb 3:1, which bestows upon Jesus the title "apostle and high priest of our confession." Clearly, this is flexible terminology that needs to be understood in its immediate context.

Why focus on the Gospel of Mark's depiction of the disciples? There are two good reasons, one disputed and one not. First, Mark is widely, although not universally, regarded as the earliest written Gospel. Moreover, it seems likely that Matthew and Luke both used some version of Mark as one of their sources. (Note that Luke 1:1–2 acknowledges an awareness of prior accounts.) This would give Mark both historical and literary primacy.

Matthew and Luke tone down Mark's often negative portrayal of the disciples. Matthew does this by showing that the disciples had at least a "little" faith and usually came to understand Jesus, if only by benefit of supplemental remedial instruction. For example, compare the teaching about "the yeast of the Pharisees" in Mark 8:14–21 and Matt 16:5–12. Mark's story ends starkly, with Jesus asking, "Do you not yet understand?" By contrast, Matthew's account explicitly says, "Then they understood. . . ." Even more striking is the story of the walking on the water in Mark 6:45–52 and Matt 14:22–33. Mark again concludes by saying the disciples did not understand, and "their hearts were hardened." (This language, taken from Isa 6:9–10, had already been used to describe *outsiders* in Mark 4:10–12.) In Matthew, however, the disciples worship Jesus, saying, "Truly, you are the Son of God!"

For his part, Luke omits some of Mark's statements about the disciples' incomprehension. He also makes a point of saying that certain things were hidden from them:

> But they did not understand this saying; its meaning was concealed from them, so that they could not perceive it. (Luke 9:45; see also 18:34)

In short, it wasn't their fault. They could not have understood what God had deliberately concealed. Comprehension came only after the resurrection, beginning with the account of the disciples on the road to Emmaus in Luke 24:13–35, from which the quotation at the heading of this chapter is taken.

The Markan Disciples

While I accept that Mark was the earliest Gospel and was used by both Matthew and Luke, I do not expect all readers to concur. That difference should not stop us from together learning what Mark may teach us about discipleship, including how to get along with fellow disciples with whom we sometimes disagree.

The second reason for focusing on Mark is that its portrayal of the disciples is by a considerable margin the most complex and ambiguous—and therefore also the most fascinating and potentially enlightening. The Markan disciples were neither heroes nor villains. To make them out to be one or the other, as interpreters occasionally have attempted, is to ignore too great a share of the evidence.[5] Rather, it is Jesus who is indisputably the hero of the

---

5. The most helpful book on this topic is C. Clifton Black, *The Disciples according to Mark: Markan Redaction in Current Debate*, 2nd ed. (Grand Rapids: Eerdmans, 2012). Black outlines three positions taken by scholars: Conservative (the disciples as heroes), Mediate (the disciples as *both* negative and positive examplars), and Liberal (the disciples as villains). The evidence he marshals in favor of the Mediate position is conclusive. See also Ernest Best, *Following Jesus:*

narrative. Just as clearly, the villains are Satan and other demonic powers. Everyone else stands somewhere on—or, in the case of the disciples, moves back and forth along—the continuum between the two.

The story started well. Jesus himself chose the Twelve, beginning with Andrew and his brother Peter (Mark 1:16).[6] Soon after, Jesus called another pair of brothers, James and John, who, like Peter and Andrew, were fishermen (Mark 1:19-20).

These four comprised the first circle of Jesus's disciples, with him from the beginning and alone mentioned in connection with Jesus's earliest ministry and first miracles (Mark 1:21-2:12) and his later "Olivet discourse" (Mark 13:3). The circle is narrowed on occasion when only Peter, James and John are mentioned, such as at the healing of Jairus's daughter (Mark 5:37) and the Transfiguration (Mark 9:2). Finally, the mercurial Peter serves as the single spokesman and eventual leader of the disciples (e.g., Mark 8:25; 9:5; 10:28; cf. Matt 16:17-19 and Gal 2:7).

The number of Jesus's followers quickly multiplied (Mark 2:18; 3:7), and he soon selected from among them a group of twelve "apostles" (Mark 3:13-19). Twelve is also the number of the tribes of Israel, and this correspondence was surely intentional. The disciples were in effect Israel in miniature. It is probable that the disciples' expectation of their eventual prominence was based partly on this fact. Indeed, in a saying found in Matt 19:28 and Luke 22:30, Jesus tells the disciples that they will one day sit on thrones, judging the twelve tribes.

The first signs of trouble are less than a chapter away. Jesus taught a large crowd by the Sea of Galilee. Afterward, he took the Twelve aside, and they inquired about the meaning of the parable of the Sower. Jesus responded, "Do you not understand this parable? Then how will you understand all the parables?" (Mark 4:13). That evening, Jesus was in a boat with the disciples. As he slept,

---

Discipleship in the Gospel of Mark (Sheffield: JSOT Press, 1981), and Hurtado, "Following Jesus," 9–29.

6. According to John 1:35–42, Andrew was a disciple of John the Baptist when he encountered Jesus, and it was he who introduced Jesus to his brother, Simon (Peter).

a "great windstorm arose" (Mark 4:37). The disciples woke Jesus and asked, "Teacher, do you not care that we are perishing?" (Mark 4:38). Jesus calmed the storm and said, "Why are you afraid? Have you still no faith?" (Mark 4:40). Not the best day's work on the part of the Twelve, and things were only just beginning.

There were ups as well as downs. According to Mark 6:7–13, Jesus sent the Twelve into the countryside to preach, cast out demons, and heal. They fulfilled their charge successfully, and, upon their return, Jesus took them away to a deserted place for rest (Mark 6:30–31). What follows immediately after, however, is the story of the feeding of the five thousand, another occasion on which the disciples appear in a less than favorable light. Once again evening comes, and with it another miracle on the Sea of Galilee. The disciples see Jesus walking on the water and are—understandably, from my limited perspective—terrified: "And they were utterly astounded, for they did not understand about the loaves, but *their hearts were hardened*" (Mark 6:51b–52).

There is no need to fill out an inning-by-inning scorecard of the disciples' performance. Suffice it to say, they did not appear to be the winning team. Worst of all, they failed dismally at the most critical moment, the end—or, at least, what seemed to be the end—when Judas betrayed and Peter denied Jesus, while the other disciples fled and hid.

The First Passion Prediction

It is most helpful to focus on the series of exchanges that lie at the heart of Mark's Gospel: the three passion predictions (that is, the three occasions on which Jesus instructed the disciples about his approaching death). It was common in antiquity for an author to employ repetition for emphasis. So it is that the story of Paul's conversion occurs three times in Acts (9:1–19; 22:1–21; 26:2–23). Likewise, the account of the conversion of the first Gentile, Cornelius, is told in Acts 10 and then repeated in step-by-step detail in Acts 11. These are critical events in the extension of the Gospel to the Gentile world, so they are repeated.

That Jesus's prediction of his death should be emphasized is unsurprising. The cross was "a stumbling block to Jews and foolishness to Gentiles" (1 Cor 1:23), the fact most in need of explanation and interpretation. But it is not all that is repeated. Following each prediction is an uncomprehending response from the disciples, and that of a particular sort. Finally, Jesus calls the disciples to himself, a signal to the reader that he intends to say something important, and teaches them about the true nature of discipleship. It is not too much to claim that understanding these three passages is the key to unlocking the entire Gospel.

The first is Mark 8:27–38, the familiar account of Peter's so-called "confession" at Caesarea Philippi. Jesus had attracted a lot of attention, and with it speculation about his mission and identity. The disciples relayed some of the most popular theories to Jesus, who then asked, "But who do you say that I am?" "You are the messiah," Peter responded (Mark 8:29).

Yes, but . . . Yes, but just what sort of messiah was he? This is the hinge in Mark's narrative, the point at which Jesus turns his face to Jerusalem and attempts to explain his fate to his closest followers:

> Then he began to teach them that the Son of Man must undergo great suffering, and be rejected by the elders, the chief priests, and the scribes, and be killed, and after three days rise again. (Mark 8:31)

Mark adds, "He said this all quite openly" (Mark 8:32). This was no parable, no "riddle, wrapped in a mystery, inside an enigma." But let's cut the disciples some slack. Jesus had just turned the world, including their own personal worlds, upside down. It could not have been easy to understand, much less to accept, what they had just heard. Imagine going in for a routine physical and being told you have a terminal illness. At first, you are dumbstruck. Then you tell the doctor, "You must be mistaken." "You can't be serious."

On the one hand, Peter did take Jesus's words seriously. On the other hand, he was sure that Jesus must be mistaken. "And Peter took him aside and began to rebuke him" (Mark 8:32). We can well imagine the substance of his reprimand. Peter was no rabbi, but he knew well enough that the messiah was to be the victor, not the victim. It was now up to Peter to reverse roles, boldly assuming the teacher's place. The passage calls to mind Jesus's rebuke of the demon in Mark 1:25. It is possible that Peter believed that this new teaching was itself a Satanic delusion.

This story follows immediately on the heels of the two-stage healing of the blind man in Mark 8:22–26. After his initial encounter with Jesus, the man could see, but only partially. People "look like trees, walking" (Mark 8:24). It took a second intervention to clarify his vision. Similarly, Peter is the half-seeing man, able to perceive Jesus's messiahship, but only dimly.

Jesus then turned and addressed the whole company of the disciples, indicating that Peter had voiced the sentiments of the entire group. "Get behind me, Satan! For you are setting your mind not on divine things but on human things" (Mark 8:33). We are reminded of yet another story, this one at the beginning of Jesus's ministry. Jesus was tempted by Satan to show himself the anticipated messiah, to fulfill human expectation, and so to bypass the cross. Peter and the other disciples now unwittingly played the tempter's role. The temptation into which they themselves had fallen is hardly unique. They wanted to use Jesus, seemingly for all the right motives.

The contrast between human and divine perspectives mentioned in this passage recurs throughout the New Testament.[7] Other early Christians treated their newfound religion as an improved means to existing ends. As we shall see, this all too human perspective required constant correction, most often through an appeal to the cross. So it is here in Mark 8:

> He called the crowd with his disciples, and said to them, "If any want to become my followers, let them deny themselves and take up their cross and follow me. For those who want to save their life will lose it, and those who lose their life for my

7. The passage echoes Isa 55:8: "My thoughts are not your thoughts, nor are your ways my ways, says the Lord."

sake, and for the sake of the gospel, will save it. For what will it profit them to gain the whole world and forfeit their life? Indeed, what can they give in return for their life?" (Mark 8:34–37)

True messiahship is thus the pattern for true discipleship. The cross is not the exception; it is the rule. Jesus addressed the crowd and said, "If any[one]," indicating that this instruction was meant for all believers and not merely the Twelve.

Mark appears to have been written during or soon after a period of persecution. If so, the choice between denying oneself and denying Christ would not have seemed metaphorical. Mark instructs believers that the present "fiery trial" (1 Pet 4:12) is to be expected. Contrary to popular belief, suffering should not be interpreted as a sign of God's rejection. Instead, it is a mark of faithfulness.

Chances are, there were failures as well as successes amongst Mark's readers. In that case, the Twelve served as prime examples of those who stumbled along the way but who ultimately would become faithful disciples after the pattern of Jesus himself.

The language of reversal is typical. To deny or "renounce" oneself is ultimately to save oneself. To attempt to gain the world is to lose it. At this point in the narrative, the disciples are well and truly in "gaining the world" mode. At the very least, the messiah was expected to be a great king who would restore Israel's fortunes. Anyone who believed that he was among that future king's closest advisors would have a difficult time not daydreaming about how his own fortunes would soon change. Consider a modern analogy: the lottery fantasy. What if you picked up what you thought was a winning ticket off the sidewalk? How would you imagine your life changing?[8] Jesus was their ticket to the top. The last thing they considered was the possibility that following him would entail a renunciation of these ambitions. Thus, their inability to understand in Mark is a moral, not an intellectual, failure. To comprehend Jesus

---

8. Funny how time alters us. Years ago, I might have imagined owning a better car or a bigger house. My fantasy now is a fully-funded retirement pension.

would be to place themselves under the hard requirement of his example.

Jesus's final statement in Mark 8 is especially poignant:

> Those who are ashamed of me and of my words in this adulterous and sinful generation, of them the Son of Man will also be ashamed when he comes in the glory of his Father with the holy angels. (Mark 8:38)

Christians in the western world probably will never be in the position to deny Jesus at the point of a sword. More likely, we will tacitly deny him at the threat of embarrassment, when the price is not our life but merely our pride. This is all the more true as the social cost of Christian discipleship rises, especially for pastors, the most publically visible churchgoers. There was a time when ministers enjoyed favored status within most communities. That is an increasingly distant—and, from the point of view of Mark, an essentially aberrant—reality.

Mark 8:27–38 establishes the pattern that we will see in the other two passion predictions:

1. *True Messiahship*
Jesus predicts his death and resurrection, revealing the unforeseen character of his messiahship. He does this forthrightly, so there is no excuse for ignorance or confusion. (See 8:31–32; 9:30–31; and 10:32–34.)

2. *False Discipleship*
The disciples do or say something that demonstrates their failure to understand Jesus and their corresponding misconstrual of their role as disciples. They still "set their minds on human things," in particular, on the attainment of higher status. (See 8:32–33; 9:32–34; and 10:35–41.)

3. *True Discipleship*
Jesus calls the disciples and, employing the language of reversal, instructs them about discipleship, which is modeled on

the paradoxical messiahship of Jesus himself. (See 8:34–38; 9:33–37; and 10:42–45.)

The Second Passion Prediction

The second passion prediction is found in Mark 9:30–37:

1. True Messiahship
They went on from there and passed through Galilee. He did not want anyone to know it; for he was teaching his disciples, saying to them, "The Son of Man is to be betrayed into human hands, and they will kill him, and three days after being killed, he will rise again." But they did not understand what he was saying and were afraid to ask him.

2. False Discipleship
Then they came to Capernaum; and when he was in the house he asked them, "What were you arguing about on the way?" But they were silent, for on the way they had argued with one another who was the greatest.

3. True Discipleship
He sat down, called the twelve, and said to them, "Whoever wants to be first must be last of all and servant of all." Then he took a little child and put it among them; and taking it in his arms, he said to them, "Whoever welcomes one such child in my name welcomes me, and whoever welcomes me welcomes not me but the one who sent me."

In hindsight, the disciples' response is almost comical. They so completely misapprehend or ignore Jesus's words that it appears reasonable to debate the question of their relative standing. When confronted, however, "they were silent." They act like a toddler caught before dinner with cookie crumbs on his chin.

Jesus knows human nature too well to say, "Whoever wishes to be first should put away such wickedness." Instead, he redirects their ambition, once again employing the language of reversal. To be somebody in God's economy, you must assume the role of nobody, a lowly servant. This is what Jesus himself already had done, but what the disciples, still hoping for a favorable outcome in Jerusalem, could not yet perceive.

Jesus then offers a demonstration, a performed parable, taking a small child in his arms. This act could symbolize adoption "since ancient adoptions sometimes included gestures of picking the child up, embracing it, or otherwise bringing it into contact with the adoptive parent's body."[9] At the very least, it represented an embrace of one who offered no advantage. Mark uses the word *paidion*, the diminutive form of *pais*, which means both "child" and "servant," linking this to the preceding verse. What servants and children had in common in antiquity was marginal social status. To welcome such a one, especially to adopt an orphaned or abandoned child, is an act of Christ-like service. The sentiment is reminiscent of Luke 6:33: "If you do good to those who do good to you, what credit is that to you? For even sinners do the same."

"Whoever welcomes one such . . . welcomes me." Greco-Roman stories sometimes included encounters with a god or hero in disguise.[10] The Old Testament mentions meetings with angels who appeared as humans (e.g., Gen 18:2–15 and 19:1–14). The New Testament book of Hebrews commands, "Do not neglect to show hospitality to strangers, for by doing that some have entertained angels without knowing it" (13:2). Mark 9:37 does not go this far, but it does build on this way of thinking. To associate with the humble, the marginal, the downtrodden is to associate with Jesus. Ironically, the disciples themselves are among those on the periphery who had been brought into the center by Jesus. In serving one another, they would be doing only what Jesus himself had already done. In effect, they could not embrace the child until they

9. Marcus, *Mark 8–16*, 675.

10. E.g., in book 1 of Homer's *Odyssey*, the goddess Athena appears in Ithaca disguised as Odysseus's friend Mentes. Allen Mandelbaum, trans., *The Odyssey of Homer* (Berkeley: University of California Press, 1990), 8–17.

realized that they themselves had been embraced. To argue who was the greatest, on the other hand, implied that their standing with Jesus was deserved.

The Third Passion Prediction

The third passion prediction is found in Mark 10:32–45. Despite their incomprehension and fear, the disciples continued to follow Jesus. Once again, he took them aside, this time describing his coming arrest and death in detail:

1. True Messiahship
See, we are going up to Jerusalem, and the Son of Man will be handed over to the chief priests and the scribes, and they will condemn him to death; then they will hand him over to the Gentiles; they will mock him, and spit upon him, and flog him, and kill him; and after three days he will rise again. (Mark 10:33–34)

"It will be 74 degrees Fahrenheit with a barometric pressure of 30.12 inches of mercury." How plain must Jesus make it? Jesus's prophecy harkens back to the description of the Suffering Servant in Isa 50:4–9 and 52:12–53:12, who is insulted, spat upon, beaten and handed over to death "for the transgression of my people" (Isa 53:8b). Furthermore, the Servant's triumph beyond death is described in Isa 53:10–12. In other words, Jesus was not telling them something they should be utterly unprepared to hear. Still, we know by now what to expect of the disciples:

2. False Discipleship
James and John, the sons of Zebedee, came forward to him and said to him, "Teacher, we want you to do for us whatever we ask of you." And he said to them, "What is it you want me to do for you?" And they said to him, "Grant us to sit, one at your right hand and one at your left, in your glory." (Mark 10:35–37)

There is disagreement as to whether the phrase "in your glory" means that the brothers now grasped that Jesus's kingship will be realized only in the eschatological future. I do not think that is the case, but it hardly matters. The point is that, as before, they are concerned with their own station. Note that it is James and John who make this extraordinarily presumptuous request ("give us *whatever* we ask"). They together with Peter have been Jesus's closest companions. As they neared Jerusalem, they sought to secure their elite status. Recall that it was Peter who was rebuked by Jesus following the first passion prediction. Now it is the turn of the other two members of that privileged in-group:

> But Jesus said to them, "You do not know what you are asking. Are you able to drink the cup that I drink, or be baptized with the baptism that I am baptized with?" They replied, "We are able." Then Jesus said to them, "The cup that I drink you will drink; and with the baptism with which I am baptized, you will be baptized; but to sit at my right hand or at my left is not mine to grant, but it is for those for whom it has been prepared." (Mark 10:38–40)

"You do not know what you are asking." I have sympathy for Zebedee's sons. I can imagine Jesus responding in the same way to my self-interested prayers. To put the best possible face on it, they wanted to be close to Jesus, but they had no idea what that entailed.

There are many layers of meaning in this text. On the surface, one might think that Jesus was speaking of his literal baptism and of a sharing in his life or blessings ("cup," as in Ps 23:5). However, the cup was often associated with suffering and judgment (e.g., Jer 49:12 and Ps 75:8), and baptism was used metaphorically to refer to immersion in some trouble or evil, as in Luke 12:50. Finally, we think of the sacraments. In that respect, all Christians, including especially Mark's own community, are questioned, "Are you able to . . . ?"

The other Old Testament text that stands behind this passage is the account of the coming of the Son of Man in "glory and kingship" in Dan 7, at which time "all peoples, nations, and languages should serve him" (Dan 7:14). The "holy ones" will share in his rule, and "all dominions shall serve and obey them" (Dan 7:27). Jesus now turns this expectation, which likely informed the request of James and John, upside down:

3. True Discipleship

When the ten heard this, they began to be angry with James and John. So Jesus called them and said to them, "You know that among the Gentiles those whom they recognize as their rulers lord it over them, and their great ones are tyrants over them. But it is not so among you; but whoever wishes to become great among you must be your servant, and whoever wishes to be first among you must be slave of all. For the Son of Man came not to be served but to serve, and to give his life a ransom for many." (Mark 10:41–45)

The indignation of the other disciples is probably not of the "righteous" variety. They might simply have been angry that James and John had tried to beat them to the top spots. Again, Jesus contrasts the human way of greatness (in this case, through the example of altogether human Gentiles) with God's way. Once more, the wish to be great is not censured; it is redirected. The language is however intensified: you must become a "servant" (*diakonos*, as in Mark 9:35) and a "slave" (*doulos*).[11] This puts the matter in the starkest terms possible.

This Son of Man "came *not* to be served but to serve . . . and to give his life a ransom for many." Jesus has merged the figures of the Son of Man and the Suffering Servant. As we shall see, the preference on the part of his followers for the first figure over the second, for glory over service, did not end with the disciples.

---

11. On the meaning of these terms, see Alberto de Mingo Kaminouchi, *"But It Is Not So Among You": Echoes of Power in Mark 10:32–45* (New York: T&T Clark, 2003), 127–39.

Everything Exactly Backwards

Mark knew that the disciples came to understand Jesus after his crucifixion and resurrection (16:7). His interest was not in their exoneration, however. The post-Easter ministry of at least some of the apostles, including their martyrdom, would likely have been known to Mark's readers. Mark instead chose to tell the backstory, in which the disciples showed themselves to be dedicated but fallible followers, perhaps much like the persons for whom this Gospel was composed.

What held back the disciples for so long? In part at least, it was their own quite natural human ambition. Their vision was distorted by their desire for earthly status. Had they seen the world as Jesus saw it, they would have realized that they had everything exactly backwards.

The first disciples were Galilean Jews who had been immersed in the same world of texts, ideas, and practices as Jesus himself. This was not the case for most believers who came after them, especially for Gentiles at home in Greco-Roman society. We should not be taken aback, therefore, to learn that these believers also could be "slow of heart," misconceiving Christian faith much as the Twelve did during the ministry of Jesus. We focus first on the group about which we know the most, the church of Corinth, founded by the apostle Paul.

CHAPTER SIX

Status Quo Corinth

First Corinthians is the quintessential Pauline letter. In it we see the apostle handling a range of issues and acting by turns as pastor, poet, preacher, and parent. This is Paul at his best: a resourceful theologian who responds imaginatively to a succession of problems and controversies. In fact, were I to retain only one of Paul's epistles in my "Desert Island Bible,"[1] this would be it.

Admittedly, some classic Pauline themes are hardly mentioned. Justification by faith, freedom from the law, and the relationship between Christianity and Judaism are issues we associate with Paul but which are almost entirely absent from this correspondence. It is simply not where the action was at Corinth. In a way, these lacunae make the letter all the more relevant and accessible to us. The issue of food laws or circumcision might not embroil your church, but the question of who gets preferential attention probably has, does, and will. Here is how Anthony Thiselton put it in his magisterial commentary:

> With today's "post-modern" mood we may compare the self-sufficient, self-congratulatory culture of Corinth coupled with an obsession about peer-group prestige, success in competition,

---

1. I am basing the idea of a "Desert Island Bible" on the popular BBC radio program, *Desert Island Discs*, in which guests are asked which eight records they would choose to take to a remote desert island.

their devaluing of tradition and universals, and near contempt for those without standing in some chosen value system. All this provides an embarrassingly close model of a postmodern context for the gospel in our own times, even given the huge historical differences and distances in so many other respects.[2]

The Surpassing Value of Honor

The classical Greek city of Corinth was largely destroyed by Rome in 146 BCE. It was re-founded a century later by Julius Caesar and colonized by Romans, many of them former slaves and, possibly, retired soldiers.[3] Its position between harbors on the Adriatic and Aegean Seas made Corinth a wealthy trading city, providing a degree of economic opportunity for the "new money," whether Romans or, over time, colonists of other nationalities. Like most of cosmopolitan Greece, it was riven between haves and have-nots. A substantial segment of the population was enslaved, and most who were not occupied the lower class of merchants, artisans, and craftspeople. In short, Corinthian society was highly stratified.[4]

New Testament scholar Wayne Meeks coined the term "status inconsistency" to describe the situation of many prominent persons at Corinth, particularly those who rose from the class of freedmen, former slaves.[5] These were the *nouveau riche* who attained their status through wealth. Such persons were in an in-

---

2. Anthony C. Thiselton, *The First Epistle to the Corinthians: A Commentary on the Greek Text*, NIGTC (Grand Rapids: Eerdmans, 2000), 16–17.

3. The former is more certain than the latter. On the composition of the Corinthian population, see Benjamin W. Millis, "The Social and Ethnic Origins of the Colonists in Early Roman Corinth," in *Corinth in Context: Comparative Studies on Religion and Society*, ed. Steven J. Friesen, Daniel N. Schowalter, and James C. Walters (Leiden: Brill, 2010), 13–35.

4. For a detailed account, see David G. Horrell, *The Social Ethos of the Corinthian Correspondence* (Edinburgh: T&T Clark, 1996).

5. Wayne A. Meeks, *The First Urban Christians: The Social World of the Apostle Paul*, 2nd ed. (New Haven: Yale University Press, 2003), 22.

herently insecure social position. Babbius, a first-century public official at Corinth, might well have been one such individual. A monument contains not one but two inscriptions identifying him as its benefactor, making it doubly certain that the public would know whom to esteem.

It is difficult to overstate the importance of social standing in the Greco-Roman world, most often calculated according to degrees of "honor" (*timē*).[6] As J. E. Lendon put it, "Honour was a filter through which the whole world was viewed, a deep structure of the Graeco-Roman mind, perhaps the ruling metaphor of ancient society."[7] Honor was very much a public acquisition. "*For Romans, being was being seen.*"[8] Because one's status was continuously scrutinized, many were "afflicted with relentless low-grade anxiety,"[9] attending to their status as one today might brood over the movements of a stock in which one had invested all of one's resources.

How did one accumulate honor? Mark T. Finney summarized "the components of life that elicited honour" as follows:

> [O]ne's birth (lineage/family/town/city); social position of friends and acquaintances; wealth; social location; the size of

6. Modern study of honor in the ancient Mediterranean world was spurred by Julian Alfred Pitt-Rivers, *The People of the Sierra* (London: Weidenfeld & Nicolson, 1954).

7. J. E. Lendon, *Empire of Honour: The Art of Government in the Roman World* (Oxford: Oxford University Press, 1997), 73. This is the classic work on honor in the Roman world. See also Richard L. Rohrbaugh, "Honor: Core Value in the Biblical World," in *Understanding the Social World of the New Testament*, ed. Dietmar Neufeld and Richard E. DeMaris (New York: Routledge, 2010), 109–25. Note Halvor Moxnes, "Honor, Shame, and the Outside World," in *The Social World of Formative Christianity and Judaism: Essays in Tribute to Howard Clark Kee*, ed. Jacob Neusner, Peder Borgen, Ernest S. Frerichs, and Richard Horsley (Philadelphia: Fortress, 1988), 207–18. Also, see David A. deSilva, *The Hope of Glory: Honor Discourse and New Testament Interpretation* (Eugene, OR: Wipf & Stock, 1999).

8. Carlin A. Barton, *Roman Honor: The Fire in the Bones* (Berkeley: University of California Press, 2001), 58 (my italics). Barton goes on to cite an example: "Cicero regretted serving in Cilicia . . . because it meant acting in squalid obscurity, far from the urban spotlight."

9. Barton, *Roman Honor*, 272.

one's retinue (soldiers/clients/slaves); and a number of miscellaneous items (clothes worn/banquets given, etc.). [10]

One's moral reputation was also a vital factor, as were, among other things, education and eloquence, military success, the holding of civic office, the provision of public beneficence, and personal appearance and health.

Thus, it is not surprising that "love of honor" (*philotimia*) was regarded by some as a cardinal virtue.[11] According to Dio Chysostom, it is the very wellspring of greatness:

> [N]either you nor any others, whether Greeks or barbarians, who are thought to have become great, advanced to glory and power for any other reason than because fortune gave to each in succession men who were jealous of honour and regarded their fame in after times as more precious than life.[12]

Interestingly, the Roman philosopher and politician Cicero described the love of honor as a natural drive:

10. Mark T. Finney, *Honour and Conflict in the Ancient World: 1 Corinthians in its Greco-Roman Social Setting* (London: Bloomsbury T&T Clark, 2012), 47. Finney's work is a superb resource for anyone wishing to learn more about ancient conceptions of honor and how they might inform one's understanding of the New Testament. Also recommend is Hellerman, *Embracing Shared Ministry*. Hellerman summarizes for a general audience his academic monograph *Reconstructing Honor in Roman Philippi* (Cambridge: Cambridge University Press, 2005) and helpfully applies his findings to the needs of today's church. On the parallel concept of "glory," see J. R. Harrison, "Paul and the Roman Ideal of Glory in the Epistle to the Romans," in *The Letter to the Romans,* ed. Udo Schnelle (Leuven: Peeters, 2009), 329–69.

11. Lenden noted that, "The gracious world of *philotimia* may in part be concealing altogether more ruthless social relations: benefactions as the ransom the rich pay for the untroubled enjoyment of their wealth" (*Empire*, 88). In short, the wealthy paid those beneath them not to disturb the social order.

Not all regarded *philotimia* positively. On differing attitudes toward "the love of honor" in ancient Greece, see Geert Roskam, Maarten De Pourcq, and Luc Van der Stockt, eds., *The Lash of Ambition: Plutarch, Imperial Greek Literature and the Dynamics of Philotimia* (Brussels: Société des Études Classiques, 2012).

12. Dio Chrysostom, *Rhod.* (*Or.* 31) 20 (Cohoon and Crosby, LCL).

Nature in fact not only puts up with but even demands it; for she offers nothing more excellent, nothing more desirable than honour, than renown, than distinction, than glory.

Nature has made us . . . enthusiastic seekers after honour, and once we have caught, as it were, some glimpse of its radiance, there is nothing we are not prepared to bear and go through in order to secure it.[13]

To the Greco-Roman mind, life was transitory, but honor eternal. The historian Livy recounted how a captured Roman soldier thrust his hand into fire, declaring to his enemy, "Look, that you may see how cheap they hold their bodies whose eyes are fixed upon renown!"[14] The Greek politician Pericles consoled Athenian parents who had lost their sons in battle with these words: "Be comforted by the fair fame of these your sons. For the love of honour alone is untouched by age, and when one comes to the ineffectual period of life [old age] it is not 'gain' as some say, that gives the greater satisfaction, but honour."[15]

Honor was widely perceived to be "a limited good." That is, "There was not enough to go around and what there was, was already all distributed. This meant that honor gained was always honor taken from another person. The result was an intense competition and envy."[16] It is not unexpected therefore that such antagonism would slither its way into the church.

Obsession with honor was present at every social level, even amongst slaves, who, although despised by their social superiors, might yet quarrel "with one another over glory and pre-eminence."[17] Seneca wrote, "You will find the slave who would rather be struck with the lash than the fist, who considers stripes and death more endurable than insulting words."[18]

---

13. Cicero, *Tusc.* 2.20.46, 2.24.58 (King, LCL).

14. Livy 2.12.13 (Foster, LCL).

15. That is, according to Thucydides, *Hist.* 2.44.4 (Smith, LCL). Compare Barton, *Roman Honor*, 11.

16. Rohrbaugh, "Honor: Core Value in the Biblical World," 112.

17. Dio Chrysostom, *2 Tars.* (*Or.* 34) 51 (Cohoon and Crosby, LCL).

18. Seneca, *Const.* 5.1 (Basore, LCL).

The poet Horace noted satirically that "Vanity [Glory] drags all, bound to her glittering car [chariot], the unknown no less than the well known."[19] We may count the residents of Corinth as among vanity's train of captives. As one scholar put it, "Corinth was a city where public boasting and self-promotion had become an art form."[20] Understandably but unfortunately, the church then as now had the habit of defaulting to the norms of its society, not least in matters of social standing.

Paul at a Disadvantage

The Corinthian mindset presented Paul with one of his greatest challenges. By his own admission, Paul was not a trained public speaker (2 Cor 11:6). He suffered by comparison with missionaries such as Apollos because, although sufficiently educated according to Jewish standards, he was no orator. The esteem in which elegant speech was held is illustrated by Paul's contemporary, the Roman rhetorician Quintilian, who wrote:

> Even though there be no hope of excelling the greatest masters of eloquence, it is yet a great honor to follow closely behind them.... from no other pursuit has greater wealth, honor, and friendship, greater present and future fame, resulted to those engaged in it, than from that of the orator.[21]

Paul was found unimposing for other reasons. He was not physically impressive (2 Cor 10:10), so he neither sounded nor looked the part of a leader. Moreover, unlike professional rhetoricians (not to mention some other apostles), he did not request payment from his audience.[22] Instead, he worked with his hands at a menial

19. Horace, *Sat.* 1.6.23–24 (Fairclough, LCL).

20. Ben Witherington III, *Conflict and Community at Corinth: A Socio-Rhetorical Commentary on 1 and 2 Corinthians* (Grand Rapids: Eerdmans, 1995), 8.

21. Quintilian, *Inst.* 12.11.29 (Russell, LCL).

22. On the social significance of apostles receiving financial support, see Bengt Holmberg, "The Methods of Historical Reconstruction in the Scholarly

occupation so that he might offer the Gospel free of charge (1 Cor 9:18). Thus, largely by deliberate choice, Paul occupied a place of low status. In consequence, some, perhaps most, above his station had difficulty taking him seriously.

To make matters worse, Paul's message was a hard sell. As we have seen, religion could be a self-centered business, focused on getting rather than giving, on short-term gains rather than long-term service. To new Christians, this religion must have seemed strange and costly, especially in its demands to de-center the ego, honor one another (including one's social inferiors), and live in a community where the least by worldly standards might be the greatest. Today, we might say that Christianity does not necessarily offer an equitable return in this life, at least in terms of material and social advancement. How then could it be a good investment?

One answer is to rearrange the balance sheet. At least some of the Corinthian Christians thought of themselves as strong, mature, wise, and gifted. By their calculation, they were successful; by Paul's, however, they were misguided, having turned aside from the word and example of Jesus, the one rejected by human authority, disdained and despised. The fact that further correspondence (2 Corinthians) was necessary shows that even Paul, for all his ingenuity and persuasiveness, could not easily win the Corinthians over to the side of the crucified Christ.

The Corinthians remind me of Hyacinth Bucket, the lead character in the BBC sitcom *Keeping Up Appearances*. Hyacinth hailed from a lower-class English family but married up to a solidly middle-class existence—and aspired to still more. She insisted on pronouncing her surname as the more elegant-sounding "Bouquet." She pompously answered the phone, "The Bouquet residence. The lady of the house speaking." She hosted elaborate candlelight suppers using her Royal Doulton china with the "hand-painted periwinkles." In short, she did everything in her power to disguise her true origins as she scaled the social ladder.

'Recovery' of Corinthian Christianity," in *Christianity at Corinth: The Quest for the Pauline Church,* ed. Edward Adams and David G. Horrell (Louisville, KY: Westminster John Knox, 2004), 255–71.

It is all here in 1 Corinthians, everything, that is, but the peri-winkles. The Corinthians were Buckets trying to pass as Bouquets. The irony, of course, is that Christ did indeed provide them a way to be significant, meaningful, valuable—important, even. Just not significant, meaningful, valuable, and important in the way they desired.

I do not for one minute believe that the Corinthians' capac-ity for both self-promotion and self-deception exceeds my own or, quite possibly, yours. Most of us play the role of poser from time to time. Like a scruffy Roman in a classic Greek city,[23] like an awkward diner at an elegant table, we need to justify our pres-ence—perhaps to others, certainly to ourselves.

Paul himself had undergone the change of perspective that he now required of the Corinthians. Years earlier, he persecuted the church, believing that Jesus was a false messiah whose crucifixion proved that he had been cursed by God (Gal 3:13). The appear-ance of the risen Lord on the road to Damascus changed not only Paul's view of Jesus; it fundamentally reversed his perception of how God works in the world. God had acted supremely through the instrument of the cross, a place of weakness, foolishness, hu-miliation, and suffering. Hence, claims to power, giftedness, and wisdom may well reveal human lostness, not divine favor. God can be most present in places of seeming abandonment (2 Cor 12:9). For Paul, the model of discipleship is unequivocally and uniquely the self-emptying of Jesus (Phil 2:5–11). At this point especially, Paul's theology aligns precisely with that of Mark's Gospel.

My Apostle is Better than Your Apostle

Paul begins his letter by confronting the Corinthians' factionalism. We might suppose that any divisions were theological in nature

---

23. "This was a city which presented itself as a new foundation while simul-taneously laying claim to the past, providing a focal point for the mixing of Greek and Roman cultures at a major crossroads in the eastern Mediterranean." Millis, "Social and Ethnic Origins," 35.

(this is the Bible, after all), but that does not appear to be the case. Instead, they were based on allegiance to specific leaders, one or another regarded as the superior brand. Here, the Corinthians sound like fan club members with a bad case of over association. It is one thing to like or even to prefer a certain singer, actor or, for that matter, pastor or teacher. It is quite another thing to merge your identity with theirs. The Corinthians' fault, like Peter's at Caesarea Philippi, was to think as humans think, not as God thinks:

> I could not speak to you as spiritual people, but rather as people of the flesh, as infants in Christ. . . . Even now you are still not ready, for you are still of the flesh. (1 Cor 3:1)

Modern readers may jump on the phrase "people of the flesh" and assume that Paul, the killjoy, must be writing about sex. Not here, at any rate. The natural impulse he wanted to challenge is something else, now quite familiar:

> For as long as there is jealousy and quarreling among you, are you not of the flesh, and behaving according to human inclinations? For when one says, "I belong to Paul," and another, "I belong to Apollos," are you not merely human? (1 Cor 3:3–4)

Think back to chapter 2. Nature may or may not lead to good ends. Natural inclinations can help us to survive, or, given free reign, can destroy both us and others. One essential function of healthy religion is the regulation of natural impulse. That is just what Paul advocates. To behave naturally is to relate to others principally according to status. One hippopotamus fights to undermine the status of another. It is only natural, for humans as for hippos. But it is not to be so among you, writes Paul.

This behavior is common, in Kansas as in Corinth. If I am brutally honest, I will admit to being more than a little Corinthian myself, especially in this respect. In my lifetime I have met several famous people and have been privileged to work with many prominent scholars and church leaders. There are times when it is appropriate or even necessary for me to mention them, but I would be fooling myself if I judged my motives invariably pure. Rooting for a winner makes us feel like a winner, and aligning ourselves with status conveys status. It is "merely human," but Paul does not regard that as an adequate standard. Indeed, God has turned human ways of reckoning on end:

> For God's foolishness is wiser than human wisdom, and God's weakness is stronger than human strength. Consider your own call, brothers and sisters: not many of you were wise by human standards, not many were powerful, not many were of noble birth. But God chose what is foolish in the world to shame the wise; God chose what is weak in the world to shame the strong; God chose what is low and despised in the world, things that are not, to reduce to nothing things that are, so that no one might boast in the presence of God. (1 Cor 1:25–29)

God chose to save through the weakness and foolishness of the cross. Also among the "low and despised" objects God chose ("called") were the Corinthians themselves, most of whom were no great shakes by conventional standards. Why then choose to pursue the very things God had shunned, to become the very sort of persons whom God had shamed? Worse still, why use the things of God to an ungodly end? This is a challenge only to those who would rely on their worthiness. To those aware of their inadequacy, this is good news indeed.

Second Corinthians 5:16 captures Paul's perspective succinctly: "From now on, therefore, we regard no one from a human point of view; even though we once knew Christ from a human point of view, we know him no longer in that way." Paul rejected the crucified Christ when at first he assessed him by human standards. Similarly, we misjudge others when we "regard them from a human point of view," determining their worth by their social standing or their utility to us.

Paul's Gifted Students

Like Jesus before him, Paul believed that God's dominion was *already* partially but *not yet* fully present. This is not an easy balance to maintain. We are wired to prefer immediate gratification. It takes a lot of effort on the part of our prefrontal cortex to defer satisfaction. On the other hand, it takes little effort to grasp why churches that emphasize present-day material prosperity attract crowds, or, for that matter, how the previously obscure 1 Chr 4:10 became a favorite verse of many contemporary Christians:

> Jabez called on the God of Israel, saying, "Oh that thou wouldst bless me and enlarge my border, and that thy hand might be with me, and that thou wouldst keep me from harm so that it might not hurt me!"

I am grateful for every blessing, and I would not mind seeing "my borders" enlarged, if that meant only having a bigger backyard. But religion that is mainly about getting is out of step with Jesus and out of balance with itself. Consider the cross and the resurrection as two poles of Christian thought. Which receives the greater attention in your church? To the extent that churches focus on the cross as the paradigm of day-to-day Christian experience, they tend to regard resurrection as a still-future reality, something Jesus alone experienced. Conversely, churches that emphasize resurrection tend to see the cross as an event in Jesus's past, something he endured so that we do not have to. We live this side of Easter, the thinking goes, and resurrection power is already available to us in tangible ways. Needless to say, where one sits on this continuum greatly influences one's perceptions about where and how God works in the world.[24]

The ideal, of course, is balance. Too much cross can lead to pessimism or despair, and too much resurrection can lead to otherworldliness or hyper-spirituality. Overall, Paul offered his read-

---

24. I discuss this subject at some length in chapter 7 of my *In God's Time: The Bible and the Future* (Grand Rapids: Eerdmans, 2002).

ers an evenhanded theology that avoided the extremes on either side. Believers do not live in a different world from that inhabited by Jesus. This is still the place of the cross. On the other hand, we witness our future in Christ's resurrection, and we experience a "foretaste" of what is to come in the presence and gifts of the Spirit (1 Cor 13:8–13).

It is telling that there is comparatively little talk of resurrection in Mark's Gospel but quite a lot of talk of the cross. Triumph over death was not a particularly challenging concept to advocate, although Gentiles might object to specifically Jewish conceptions of resurrection (Acts 17:32). Nor did prosperity require a slick sales pitch. The disciples balked instead at the cross. Likewise, the Corinthians were "all in" for present-day empowerment plus the promise of eternal life. Indeed, Paul's argument in 1 Cor 15 might indicate that some Corinthians believed they *already* had been raised to new life and required no future physical resurrection. To counter this way of thinking, Paul refers them repeatedly to the cross, to the *not yet* side of the ledger. He most pointedly contrasts their way of thinking with his perspective in 1 Cor 4:8–10:[25]

> Already you have all you want! Already you have become rich! Quite apart from us you have become kings! Indeed, I wish that you had become kings, so that we might be kings with you! For I think that God has exhibited us apostles as last of all, as though sentenced to death, because we have become a spectacle to the world, to angels and to mortals. We are fools for the sake of Christ, but you are wise in Christ. We are weak, but you are strong. You are held in honor, but we in disrepute.

Already the Corinthians have all they want, thinking themselves rich, royal, wise, strong, and honorable. There is nothing inherently wrong with this wish list—that is, if viewed in the proper perspective. For example, Paul himself admits to possessing and teaching a kind of wisdom:

---

25. David Horrell provides an extended discussion of this and similar passages in *The Social Ethos*, 199–237 ("Conflict at Corinth and Apostolic Lifestyle").

Yet among the mature we do impart wisdom, although it is not a wisdom of this age or of the rulers of this age, who are doomed to pass away. (1 Cor 2:6)

"Not . . . of this age" is the caveat. Unfortunately, what the Corinthians were after belonged very much to this age. By that standard, the apostles were pitiable failures, rather like prisoners of war who marched at the end of the victor's parade, objects of derision who awaited execution. This is extreme language, but Paul is attempting something extremely difficult: to turn the Corinthians' world upside down as his own had been en route to Damascus. He goes on to describe the life of an apostle, which is anything but comfortable and glamorous:

To the present hour we are hungry and thirsty, we are poorly clothed and beaten and homeless, and we grow weary from the work of our own hands. When reviled, we bless; when persecuted, we endure; when slandered, we speak kindly. We have become like the rubbish of the world, the dregs of all things, to this very day. (1 Cor 4:11–13)

This passage reminds me of an impassioned lecture I once heard by Tony Campolo, a Christian scholar and speaker. To paraphrase: if faithfulness to God can be measured by material blessing, what are we to make of the Christians of Haiti, whose discipleship far outshines our own but who live in abject poverty? This is strong medicine, but self-justification is a deep infection.

We have noted Paul's theological equilibrium, and 1 Cor 4:8–13 shows us only one side, the corrective side, of his thinking. In effect, the Corinthians had taken the half of Paul's message they liked and made it the whole. Paul himself believed that the Spirit empowered Christians with "gifts," such as prophecy, discernment, and healing (1 Cor 12:8–10), and enabled them to bear "fruit," including kindness, peace and patience (Gal 5:22–23). More significant still, he believed that God in Christ had already made of Jews and Gentiles one new people. That meant that the boundary markers that had distinguished Jews from Gentiles—namely, circumcision, food laws, and the observance of special days—were no longer obligatory. This is a radical change indeed, and it shows that Paul did believe that some things had categorically altered as a result of Christ.

By all accounts, spiritual gifts were distributed liberally amongst the Corinthians. Like persons employing chess pieces as checkers, however, they did not know how to think about what they had been given, and so they defaulted to playing the familiar game. Spiritual endowments became status markers, especially the esoteric gift of speaking in tongues. Paul's response is both reasoned and revealing. First, he makes it clear that these are gifts, not rewards: "What do you have that you did not receive? And if you received it, why do you boast as if it were not a gift?" (1 Cor 4:7b). You may as well boast of being born.

To Each is Given

Paul's second argument is that all believers, not just an elite few, are so gifted: "*to each* is given the manifestation of the Spirit. . . . All these are activated by one and the same Spirit, who allots *to each one individually* just as the Spirit chooses" (1 Cor 12:7b, 11; see also 7:7). Here is the clincher: "to each is given . . . *for the common good*" (1 Cor 12:7). There is therefore no ground for jealousy. The gift given one benefits all, and all require the gifts given others. It is rather like a church potluck or bring-and-share supper. All benefit from the varied abilities of each. Indeed, the more varied the abilities, the better the supper. Thirty Jello-O salads doth not a potluck make. Of course, humans being human, even a bring-and-share can turn into a bring-and-compare. Corinth tempts us all.

It is in this context that Paul offers one of his best-known images: the church as the Body of Christ (1 Cor 12:12–31). All parts of the body are necessary to and benefit the whole. "If one member suffers, all suffer together with it; *if one member is honored, all rejoice together with it.*" The body metaphor would have been familiar to ancient readers, but the lessons Paul drew from it would not. Typically, it was employed "to urge those of the lower classes to respect and value their place in the current social order and not to disrupt the 'natural equilibrium' of the 'body' by rebelling against their superiors."[26] Paul turns that body, as it were, on its head.

Many years ago, I worked on the staff of a marvelously gifted senior pastor. He was the best week-by-week preacher I have ever heard, but he was also the most generous at sharing his pulpit with others. I have also known (though not worked with) a few pastors who seemed determined that no one, especially no one on their staff, should outshine them. The willingness to share credit and to rejoice in the successes of others is one of the surest markers of genuine spirituality. Paul here reminds me of my own father, who loved to quote the Harry Truman saying "It's amazing what you can accomplish if you do not care who gets the credit."

Throughout 1 and 2 Corinthians, Paul advances a "communitarian ethic" in which the individual is called upon to put others, especially those with fewer advantages, ahead of self. He summarizes his attitude in 1 Cor 10:33: "I try to please everyone in everything I do, not seeking my own advantage, but that of many, so that they may be saved."

We see this perspective manifested in his discussion of the Lord's Supper in 1 Cor 11:17–34, wherein the wealthy are required to defer to the poor. It is also evident in Paul's statements regarding food sacrificed to idols: the self-styled "strong" are charged to attend first to the sensibilities of the "weak" (1 Cor 8). Finally, he employs the same logic in chapter 14 to deflate the pretentions of those who speak in tongues. A gift is not to be valued according to its scarcity or obscurity. Rather, the measure of its worth is the extent to which it builds up the whole Christian community. By that standard, speaking in tongues is a secondary, although still respected, spiritual endowment.

Paul's masterstroke comes in chapter 13. So, you want spiritual gifts, do you? Then seek to possess the best of all: love. This move brilliantly undercuts all claims to superiority. The highest spirituality is manifested by those who are "not envious or boastful or arrogant" (1 Cor 13:4). Moreover, the very spiritual gifts in which the Corinthians glory are those that are destined to pass

26. Finney, *Honour and Conflict*, 182.

away. They are only temporary, even childish expedients (1 Cor
13:8–11). "And now faith, hope, and love abide, and the greatest of
these is love" (1 Cor 13:13). It is acceptable to want the greatest gift,
and that very gift will empower you to put aside striving and live
in harmony with, not above, others.

To Boast or Not to Boast

Various forms of the word "boast"[27] have appeared in the quotations cited above. It is a common and distinctive Pauline word,
employed over fifty times in cognate forms in his letters.[28] In the
passages mentioned above, boasting is equivalent to self-glorifi-
cation, or as we would say today, bragging. Bragging about one's
associations, gifts or, especially, attainments (one's "works," to use
Paul's terminology) is precisely the kind of naked self-justification
Paul challenged. If one is justified by Christ, then one can make
no claim to justify oneself. In that way, believing in Christ and
boasting in self are antithetical exercises. Paul puts it this way
in Rom 3:27: "Then what becomes of boasting? It is excluded. By
what law? By that of works? No, but by the law of faith."

That is not all there is to it. On numerous occasions, Paul
employs the same terms favorably. For example, in 2 Cor 7:4a he
writes, "I often boast about you," and in 1:12, "Indeed, this is our
boast, the testimony of our conscience: we have behaved in the
world with frankness and godly sincerity, not by earthly wisdom
but by the grace of God—and all the more toward you." Paul's

27. The primary noun is *kauchēsis* and the verb *kauchasthai*.
28. See Timothy B. Savage, *Power through Weakness: Paul's Understanding of
the Christian Ministry in 2 Corinthians* (Cambridge: Cambridge University Press,
2004), 54–64; Duane F. Watson, "Paul and Boasting," in *Paul in the Greco-Roman
World: A Handbook,* ed. J. Paul Sampley (Harrisburg, PA: Trinity, 2003), 77–100;
Andrew D. Clarke, *Secular and Christian Leadership in Corinth: A Socio-Historical
and Exegetical Study of 1 Corinthians 1–6* (Eugene, OR: Wipf & Stock, 2006), 95–99;
and Jan Lambrecht, "Dangerous Boasting: Paul's Self-commendation in 2 Corinthians 10–13," in *The Corinthian Correspondence,* ed. Reimund Bieringer (Leuven:
Leuven University Press, 1996), 325–46.

usage is therefore complicated and requires a somewhat fuller explanation. When is it proper for Paul—and by extension, for us—to "boast?"

The Septuagint, the Greek translation of the Old Testament, uses the same words both negatively and positively. An example of the former is Ps 49:5–6:

> Why should I fear on an evil Day? The lawlessness at my heel will surround me—those who trust in their power and boast of the abundance of their riches.[29]

In Judg 7:2, Gideon is told to reduce the size of his army; otherwise, Israel would boast that it defeated the Midianites by its own power. Similarly, Prov 20:9 claims that no one may boast of having a pure heart. On the other hand, one is enjoined to boast or "exult" in the Lord in Ps 5:11:

> And let all who hope in you be glad; forever they will rejoice, and you will encamp among them, and those who love your name will boast in you.

It is instructive that in writing to the Corinthians, Paul twice quotes Jer 9:23–24:[30]

> This is what the Lord says: Let not the wise boast in his wisdom, and let not the mighty boast in his might, and let not the wealthy boast in his wealth, but let him who boasts boast in this: that he understands and knows that I am the Lord.

This verse helps to explain Paul's varied usage. To boast in one's attainments as if they were the basis for one's right standing, one's justification, is wrong. It is right, however, to "boast" in God and,

---

29. Translations from the Septuagint are taken from Albert Pietersma and Benjamin G. Wright, eds., *A New English Translation of the Septuagint* (Oxford: Oxford University Press, 2007). The citations of verses correspond to the NRSV.

30. 1 Cor 1:31 and 2 Cor 10:17.

by extension, in God's works. Admittedly, the latter presents a slippery slope. Boasting in what God has done through or for oneself may cloak self-promotion. Paul was aware of the problem. In 2 Cor 10:13 he writes, "We, however, will not boast beyond limits, but will keep within the field that God has assigned to us, to reach out even as far as you." He could justly take satisfaction in what God had done within the sphere of his given apostleship, which included the founding of the Corinthian church. Once again, we find a helpful balance in Paul. He does not say that we must think ourselves useless and thus find no fulfillment in our work. At the same time, we are not to think of ourselves too highly (Rom 12:3); instead, we are to "love one another with mutual affection; [and to] *outdo one another in showing honor*" (Rom 12:10). (Note how love and mutuality necessitate a new distribution of honor.) What Paul cannot abide is an attempt either to position oneself above others or to locate oneself beyond the need of grace.

Still, it is a tricky business, both because of the human tendency to self-deception and because of the differing perceptions and motives of others. An arrogant word may be veiled with innocence, and an innocent word may be judged as arrogance. Paul himself struggled with similar distinctions in 2 Corinthians, where he found it necessary to boast "according to human standards" and "as a fool" in order to get through to his obdurate readers.[31] Indeed, 2 Cor 10–13 contains the highest concentration of "boasting" language in the entire Bible. It is also one of the most personal and combative sections of any New Testament epistle. If we liken the Corinthian letters to a boxing match (not an altogether unfitting comparison), these would be the decisive final rounds, and they deserve special attention for the purpose of this study.

If at First . . .

One of my favorite pieces of light reading is Stephen Pile's 1979 *The Book of Heroic Failures*, a collection of humorous stories

---

31. E.g., 2 Cor 11:18 and 11:17.

about gross ineptitude and remarkably bad luck. (Ironically, the book went on to become a bestseller, breaking Pile's own streak of losses.) Paul was anything but inept, of course, and luck is a disputable theological category. Still, we might well regard 1 Corinthians as a heroic failure. It is wonderful, even luminous, but it did not resolve the fundamental problem at Corinth. If anything, the situation appears to have gotten worse.

It is impossible to know in detail what happened next. Much of the uncertainty is due to questions about the nature of 2 Corinthians. The letter jumps abruptly from one tone and agenda to another. In 2 Cor 1:1-2:13, Paul describes a "painful visit" and expresses his relief at the Corinthians' subsequent repentance. At the conclusion of this section he writes:

> When I came to Troas to proclaim the good news of Christ, a door was opened for me in the Lord; but my mind could not rest because I did not find my brother Titus there. So I said farewell to them and went on to Macedonia. (2 Cor 2:12–13)

Five chapters later, the story picks up right where it left off in 2:13:

> For even when we came into Macedonia, our bodies had no rest, but we were afflicted in every way—disputes without and fears within. But God, who consoles the downcast, consoled us by the arrival of Titus, and not only by his coming, but also by the consolation with which he was consoled about you, as he told us of your longing, your mourning, your zeal for me, so that I rejoiced still more. (2 Cor 7:5–16)

Most jarring of all is the unexpected shift to polemic in chapters 10-13, which contain some of the harshest language in any of Paul's letters, a far cry from the consolation and rejoicing of chapter 7.

Some have argued that Paul simply addressed different groups at Corinth at different moments in the letter. That seems improbable, although it is not impossible. Two other explanations are more widely held by scholars. The first is that the letter was written over a period of time during which the situation at Corinth changed. The second hypothesis is that 2 Corinthians contains elements of as many as six originally separate pieces of correspondence. Both approaches have something in common: neither attempts to read the letter as a single sustained argument. A major difference is chronology. Those of the single-letter persuasion draw the order of events from the existing arrangement of the letter, while those of the latter view construct from the various bits what seems the most plausible chronology.

Given these complications, we shall focus on a few central and mostly uncontested points. The first is obvious to even the most casual observer: trouble continued at Corinth. Paul returned after writing 1 Corinthians but met with resistance, particularly from some unnamed individual (2 Cor 2:5–11). His plans for a subsequent visit fell through, which encouraged doubts about his sincerity (2 Cor 1:15–22). At some point during his absence, other Christian leaders, whom Paul derisively termed "super apostles," arrived to find a ready audience at Corinth. They took payment for their teaching and seemed more impressive and credentialed than the church's lowly founder. It is their claims that Paul counters most forcefully in chapters ten to thirteen.[32]

A second indisputable point is that Paul felt the need to shore up his apostolic authority. He already had laid claim to the Corinthians' affections and obedience as their church's founding father (1 Cor 4:15), and again he mentioned his direct commissioning by Christ (1:1 in both epistles). But the approach that dominates this letter is an appeal to character, specifically to the myriad afflictions and losses he endured for the sake of Christ.

---

32. See, for example, V. Henry T. Nguyen, *Christian Identity in Corinth: A Comparative Study of 2 Corinthians, Epictetus and Valerius Maximus*, WUNT 2.243 (Tübingen: Mohr Siebeck, 2008), 194–203 ("The Subversive Christ-Like Identity [2 Cor 10–13]").

Trouble Comes in Threes

Second Corinthians contains three extremely impressive catalogs of the sufferings Paul bore as a missionary (2 Cor 4:7–10; 6:3–10; and 11:23–33). As with the three passion predictions in Mark, each subsequent description is longer and more detailed than the one before it. The case is made then pressed harder and harder still. The first of these descriptions is the most familiar:

> But we have this treasure in clay jars, so that it may be made clear that this extraordinary power belongs to God and does not come from us. We are afflicted in every way, but not crushed; perplexed, but not driven to despair; persecuted, but not forsaken; struck down, but not destroyed; always carrying in the body the death of Jesus, so that the life of Jesus may also be made visible in our bodies. (2 Cor 4:7–10)

Chances are you have heard at least one sermon about treasure in clay jars. It is a memorable image that makes Paul's point concisely. In verse 5, Paul had written, "we do not proclaim ourselves; we proclaim Jesus Christ as Lord and ourselves as your slaves for Jesus's sake." "It is not about us," in other words. What authenticates Paul's mission is not his own excellence. He is not the treasure, and it is a mistake to look to other leaders as if they were. Paul's "clayness," his servanthood, is apparent in his weakness, his lowliness, but it is through these that God's power is at work. Moreover, suffering for Christ is evidence of identity with Christ. Paul's attitude is reminiscent of that of the apostles in Acts 5:41, who "rejoiced that they were considered worthy to suffer *dishonor* for the sake of the name." Half-hearted allegiance merits only half-hearted opposition, if that.

The phrase "carrying in the body the death of Jesus" should not be interpreted to mean that Paul had a martyr theology or a death wish. Paul followed a crucified Lord who was himself a servant. He lived under the same imperium as Jesus and endured its same rejection. But "we do not lose heart" (2 Cor 4:1). Paul is undefeated; in and through his frail body, the resurrection life of Jesus is already present, fueling hope and supplying endurance.

Paul's argument resembles what we saw earlier in 1 Cor 4:8–13 ("We have become like the rubbish of the world"). Once more, Paul argues against the grain of Corinthian culture. What to Paul is a proof of his apostleship is to the Corinthians a demerit if not a disqualification. It is instructive—and not a little painful—to see how difficult it was to get the Corinthians to see the world as Paul did, through the lens of the cross. If this sounds a lot like Jesus's struggles with the disciples, it is because it is.

Second Corinthians 6:3–10 makes the case again and at greater length that "as servants of God we have commended ourselves in every way" (2 Cor 6:4). What sort of commendation does Paul make? As a charismatic personality? A riveting public speaker? A leading intellectual? No, but "through great endurance, in afflictions, hardships, calamities, beatings, imprisonments, riots, labors, sleepless nights, [and] hunger" (2 Cor 6:4b–5). This time, however, Paul adds a list of positive attributes: "by purity, knowledge, patience, kindness, holiness of spirit, genuine love, [and] truthful speech" (2 Cor 6:6–7a). Favorable though these may be, they are not on the list of most desired leadership qualities, at least as Corinthian society ranked them. True, Paul then adds "and the power of God," but this he immediately qualifies by including a list much like that in chapter 4:

> In honor and dishonor, in ill repute and good repute. We are treated as impostors, and yet are true; as unknown, and yet are well known; as dying, and see—we are alive; as punished, and yet not killed; as sorrowful, yet always rejoicing; as poor, yet making many rich; as having nothing, and yet possessing everything. (6:7b–10)

It is glorious theology, and it was not working, at least not for some.[33]

Paul's third and longest list of apostolic misfortunes is found

---

33. We have no way of knowing how much of the Corinthian congregation was disaffected at any given time. It might well have been a small minority, but, if so, it was an influential minority whom Paul felt compelled to correct.

in 2 Cor 11:22–33, which brings us to a final point on which most interpreters agree: the situation at Corinth took a turn for the worse, and Paul at last decided to change tactics. His response is found in chapters 10-13, which comprise a distinct unit, whether composed as a separate epistle or as a response appended to an existing letter. [34]

The Problem with Self-Promotion

We noted earlier the many references to boasting in these chapters. Chapter 10 makes the distinction between rightful and wrongful boasting, concluding:

> "Let the one who boasts, boast in the Lord." For it is not those who commend themselves that are approved, but those whom the Lord commends. (2 Cor 11:17–18)

Chapter 11 makes clear that it is the "super" (*hyper*) apostles who have successfully "commended themselves" to the young church: "such boasters are false apostles, deceitful workers, disguising themselves as apostles of Christ" (2 Cor 11:13). They "boast according to human standards" (2 Cor 11:18), appealing to the Corinthians' vanity. They thus personify and amplify the very error Paul had labored to correct in 1 Corinthians—and Jesus had attempted to correct at Caesarea Philippi ("you are setting your mind not on divine things but on human things;" Mark 8:33b).

My mother was a nutritionist and at one time even had a televised cooking show. Nevertheless, she was no match for the guy with the ice cream truck, especially when she was away at work and there was loose cash to be found. Similarly, Paul's absence

34. See J. Paul Sampley's analysis of Paul's rhetorical strategy in his "Paul, His Opponents in 2 Corinthians 10–13, and the Rhetorical Handbooks," in *The Social World of Formative Christianity and Judaism: Essays in Tribute to Howard Clark Kee*, ed. Jacob Neusner et al (Philadelphia: Fortress, 1988), 162–77.

made the appeal of these interlopers to his neighborhood all but irresistible.

Paul regarded his opponents' blatant self-promotion as utter foolishness, wholly unlike the character of Jesus, but it was just the sort of foolishness for which the Corinthians proved a willing audience. So, with great reluctance and accompanied by a long string of caveats, Paul finally engaged them on their own ground. His discomfort is palpable. This is a lunatic defense, but it is what the court's insane rules of evidence required:

> What I am saying in regard to this boastful confidence, I am saying not with the Lord's authority, but as a fool; since many boast according to human standards, I will also boast. . . . But whatever anyone dares to boast of—I am speaking as a fool—I also dare to boast of that. Are they Hebrews? So am I. Are they Israelites? So am I. Are they descendants of Abraham? So am I. Are they ministers of Christ? I am talking like a madman—I am a better one. (2 Cor 11:17–18, 21b–23a)

Having made this unhappy concession, Paul returns to form. What truly makes him a better minister of Christ? He answers by enumerating his sufferings for the third time:

> With far greater labors, far more imprisonments, with countless floggings, and often near death. Five times I have received from the Jews the forty lashes minus one. Three times I was beaten with rods. Once I received a stoning. Three times I was shipwrecked; for a night and a day I was adrift at sea. (2 Cor 11:23b–25; the list goes on through verse 29)

Next, he returns to the theme of boasting, again attempting to overturn convention:

> If I must boast, I will boast of the things that show my weakness. The God and Father of the Lord Jesus (blessed be he forever!) knows that I do not lie. In Damascus, the governor under King Aretas guarded the city of Damascus in order to seize me,

but I was let down in a basket through a window in the wall, and escaped from his hands. (2 Cor 11:30–33)

Paul is no Titan, no superhero. His surreptitious departure from Damascus was humiliating and would have been regarded by others as shameful (that is, dishonorable). It was the first time Paul's life had been threatened, and it left a vivid impression. Acts 9:25 adds a further detail: the escape occurred under cover of darkness. Paul's opponents might have recounted the story as evidence of his cowardice. It is possible that Paul himself deliberately contrasted his behavior with that of the courageous Roman soldier awarded the *corona muralis*, the "wall crown," for being the first to scale an enemy's wall during battle.[35] In any case, Paul used the episode to dramatize his point that it is God in whom he may justly boast. It is hard to see God at work where human strength appears a sufficient agency. For that reason, Paul would instead highlight his weakness, his insufficiency, to demonstrate the authenticity of his ministry.[36] What has been achieved, including the establishment of the church at Corinth, was accomplished by God's power. Paul's apostleship is validated by the strange but beautiful calculus of the cross.

Much the same line of argument occurs in chapter 12. Paul first reengages the Corinthians on their home turf: "It is necessary to boast; nothing is to be gained by it, but I will go on to visions and revelations of the Lord" (2 Cor 12:1). Paul reluctantly concedes that he must boast if he is to be granted a hearing. The issue is not pedigree but spiritual experience, which Paul's opponents must have claimed in abundance. At least two problems are inherent in any such assertion. First, at best it is God who grants and enables the experience; hence, it is not necessarily a sign of individual merit. Second, such occurrences are impossible to validate. Anyone can claim to have had a profound mystical experience. Those that are

35. E. A. Judge, "The Conflict of Educational Aims in New Testament Thought," *Journal of Christian Education* 9 (1966): 44–45.

36. See the fine study by David Alan Black, *Paul, Apostle of Weakness: Astheneia and Its Cognates in the Pauline Literature*, rev. ed. (Eugene, OR: Pickwick, 2012).

not blatant fabrications might still be attributable to any number of alternative causes ranging from delusion to indigestion.

Still, Paul proceeds, albeit in the third person, which creates rhetorical distance between Paul the letter writer and Paul the visionary:

> I know a person in Christ who fourteen years ago was caught up to the third heaven—whether in the body or out of the body I do not know; God knows ... [he] was caught up into Paradise and heard things that are not to be told, that no mortal is permitted to repeat. On behalf of such a one I will boast, but on my own behalf I will not boast, except of my weaknesses. (2 Cor 12:2, 4–5)

First Kings 8:27 refers literally to "heaven and the heaven of heavens," on the basis of which some "rabbis deduced that there were three heavens," the third being the highest and so the most holy.[37] The essential point is that should Paul choose to play their game, he could trump whatever card his opponents held. It is noteworthy that the incident Paul mentions occurred fourteen years earlier. Paul was no ecstatic come lately, and if he had waited this long to tell the Corinthians about his vision, his disclosure here is all the more potent. It is as if a venerable public official had been accused of being unpatriotic by an upstart political rival. Under duress, the senior leader produces his Congressional Medal of Honor. Paul held the "high ground," and his adversaries had failed dismally at the task of opposition research. Paul goes on:

> But if I wish to boast, I will not be a fool, for I will be speaking the truth. But I refrain from it, so that no one may think better of me than what is seen in me or heard from me, even considering the exceptional character of the revelations. (2 Cor 12:6–7a)

The proof is in the serving; actions speak louder than boasts.

---

37. Murray J. Harris, *The Second Epistle to the Corinthians. A Commentary on the Greek Text*, NIGTC (Grand Rapids: Eerdmans, 2005), 840.

Power in Weakness

As he did in the previous chapter, Paul concludes a section in which he reluctantly boasts about his up-to-the-Corinthian-standard credentials with a longer account of his weakness:[38]

> Therefore, to keep me from being too elated, a thorn was given me in the flesh, a messenger of Satan to torment me, to keep me from being too elated. Three times I appealed to the Lord about this, that it would leave me, but he said to me, "My grace is sufficient for you, for power is made perfect in weakness." (2 Cor 12:7b–9a)

Centuries of speculation have not yielded certainty about the nature of Paul's "thorn in the flesh." The likeliest candidate seems to be a physical malady, perhaps eye disease (see Gal 4:15 and 6:11). Such bodily limitation would have been evident to all, and thus another source of humiliation, and it would help to account for Paul's less than imposing physical presence. The exalted "third heaven" is echoed in Paul's threefold request for relief, which itself recalls Jesus's threefold temptation in the wilderness (Matt 4:1–11) and threefold prayer in Gethsemane (Matt 26:36–46). The thorn was necessary, Paul recounts, to keep him from becoming elated, so that he might in fact be more pliable, more available, and more perfectible. Or, we might paraphrase Paul this way: we can be filled by God only to the extent that we are not already full of ourselves.

> So, I will boast all the more gladly of my weaknesses, so that the power of Christ may dwell in me. Therefore I am content with weaknesses, insults, hardships, persecutions, and calamities for the sake of Christ; for whenever I am weak, then I am strong. (2 Cor 12:9b–10)

The letter's concluding paragraph sums up Paul's teaching:

---

38. For Old Testament parallels, see Savage, *Power through Weakness*, 167–71.

> Finally, brothers and sisters, farewell. Put things in order, listen to my appeal, agree with one another, live in peace; and the God of love and peace will be with you. (2 Cor 13:11)

Their fellowship is to embody essential attributes of God: love and peace. The first is key to the second. Paul had already written them that "love is not envious or boastful or arrogant" (1 Cor 13:4b). Now was the time to put that instruction more fully into practice and so to live at peace with one another.

The Corinthian Mirror

It appears that Paul made a final trip to Corinth during which he wrote the epistle to the Romans (Rom 15:25–27 and Acts 20:1–3). Many of the concerns that prompted 1 and 2 Corinthians remained on Paul's mind as he wrote the Roman Christians, most of whom he had never met. It is evident that Paul believed the lessons taught at Corinth were relevant elsewhere. Note for example the many now familiar themes found in Rom 12:

> Do not be conformed to this world, but be transformed by the renewing of your minds . . . [do] not think of yourself more highly than you ought to think, but . . . think with sober judgment, each according to the measure of faith that God has assigned. For as in one body we have many members, and not all the members have the same function, so we, who are many, are one body in Christ, and individually we are members one of another. . . . love one another with mutual affection; outdo one another in showing honor. . . . Live in harmony with one another; do not be haughty, but associate with the lowly; do not claim to be wiser than you are. . . . If it is possible, so far as it depends on you, live peaceably with all. . . . Do not be overcome by evil, but overcome evil with good. (Rom 12:2a, 3b–5, 10, 16, 18, 21)

Given this final visit, it is reasonable to conclude that Paul ultimately succeeded in winning over at least a sizeable majority of the cantankerous Corinthian congregation. If he had failed to do so, it is unlikely that his letters would have been preserved and distributed. We would be much the poorer for that loss.

Few things make me happier as a New Testament professor than hearing students say that they have become excited about Paul for the first time. I do not mean to imply that Paul is a cuddly, unchallenging, uncontroversial figure. Hardly! There is a spiritual depth in him rarely seen, and it resonates at a critical frequency with the perspective of Jesus himself. We might not approximate it, but we can at least appreciate and emulate it.

The Corinthian letters are a matchless resource for reflection on congregational life, a revealing mirror to hold up to our churches today. Naturally, the lessons we draw will vary with our circumstances. Being ordained myself, I am most struck by the fact that Paul thought it necessary in the end to present credentials the Corinthians were prepared to recognize. He did much the same thing in the other epistle in which he vigorously defended his authority, the letter to the Galatians (1:1-2:14). These examples raise a vital question: what *should* and what actually *does* authorize ministry today? Some of Paul's readers sought to replicate the Corinthian status hierarchy within their church. Leaders who played their game fit in seamlessly and were rewarded accordingly. Paul on the other hand labored to initiate the Corinthians into an alternative reality that, among other things, validated the leadership of a servant. Many contemporary pastors might sympathize with Paul. They do the often gritty, grinding daily work of ministry but may look small and unimportant when compared to a glitzy celebrity preacher.

Many other questions arise that are pertinent to all Christians. Who is honored and on what basis? Do the prominent and the wealthy exercise undue influence and receive excessive attention in our churches? Are the marginalized of society also marginalized in our congregations? Do those of lower status feel welcome? In short, do our churches look more like the city of Corinth or more like the dominion of God?

CHAPTER SEVEN

Saints Elsewhere

Like death and taxes, status conflicts are an undesirable inevitability. We may assume that no human community ever existed that did not experience at least some tensions of this kind. This is as true of the first as of the twenty-first century church. Christians are human, and humans are natively status conscious. With respect to the fact that we are meaning-seeking creatures, this is an inherently productive capacity. With respect to the fact that we are inclined to seek meaning at the expense of others, it is inherently problematic.

Paul was only one of many early church leaders, all of whom had the job of helping communities of believers to conceptualize a reality within which their being together—productively, harmoniously, *Christianly*—made sense. It is not the purpose of this short book to catalog every relevant instruction found in the pages of the New Testament. Instead, the goal is to encourage Christians to read Scripture with heightened awareness of these issues and thereby to appropriate its lessons for themselves—to conceptualize their own reality differently, in other words.

To that end, we have focused attention on Jesus, the disciples, and the Christian community about which we have the most information, the church at Corinth. This chapter rounds out our study by considering a handful of other New Testament texts, specifically, five representative letters written to assist and to challenge early Christian communities.

Philippians

Paul's problems were not limited to Corinth. We have already mentioned the church of Philippi, whom the apostle admonished, "Let the same mind be in you that was in Christ Jesus, who, though he was in the form of God, did not regard equality with God as something to be exploited, but emptied himself."

The church in the Macedonian city of Philippi was especially dear to Paul. It was the first congregation he established in Europe, and it actively supported his missionary work. Paul now wrote to them from prison, which gives his remarks special poignancy and urgency. He did not know whether he would be released, languish in prison, or be executed (Phil 1:20–26). Like an aged parent anxious for family harmony, Paul was concerned that this beloved community not be tarnished by jealousies or divisions.

Early in the letter, Paul referred cryptically to "some who proclaim Christ from envy and rivalry . . . out of selfish ambition" (Phil 1:15a, 17a). The word translated "selfish ambition" is derived from the Greek *eritheia,* which originally referred to a hired day laborer and then, by extension, to one who sought public office for private gain. (That semantic shift vividly illustrates the scorn of the upper class for manual labor.) It thus came to mean base and contemptible self-seeking, a willingness to do anything for personal advancement, much as we speak of someone "prostituting himself" today. No one knows to what or whom Paul refers, and as is always true in such cases, uncertainty opens the field to endless and largely pointless conjecture. What can be stated categorically is that Paul did not want this attitude to infect the Philippians. He used the same word again in the next chapter, in the section immediately preceding the "Christ hymn" of Phil 2:6–11: "Do nothing from *selfish ambition* or conceit, but in humility regard others as better than yourselves. Let each of you look not to your own interests, but to the interests of others" (Phil 2:3–4).

As with the categories "service" and "crucifixion," Paul turns a negative, "humility," into a positive. "'Humility' was an inflammatory term already in classical antiquity, a culture that was oriented to the ideal of the free man and of his honor."[1] To be humble was to be servile and weak. By contrast, Paul and other New Testament authors commend humility as a cardinal virtue. Of course, what they had in mind was neither a hypocritical false modesty, nor an unhealthy self-deprecation, nor an unjust subjugation. Instead, the humility they enjoined was, in the words of biblical scholar Reinhard Feldmeier, an "orientation of existence and of conduct that restrains oneself to the benefit of the other person."[2] That is why love and humility are so often associated, as indeed they are here in Phil 2:2–3: "having the same love . . . in humility."

All that being said, to "regard [all] others as better than yourselves" might still seem an objectionable, even an intolerable command. By no reasonable measure is any—let alone each—of us the worst person in the world. Is self-flagellation the way to godliness after all?

The key term is "regard" (*hēgeisthai*), which may also be translated "deem," "reckon," or "count." We are to act toward others as we would act in the presence of superiors. Specifically, this means looking to their interests, to their needs, to their comfort. Even a thoroughly selfish person is likely to behave hospitably toward a highly honored guest. On the other hand, most of us have had the experience of appearing "invisible," that is, of being overlooked, regarded almost as a piece of furniture, in the presence of more eminent persons. Between high school and college, I worked as a page in the Illinois Senate. One quickly learned which senators saw the pages as individuals, treating them with some respect, and which looked right through them. In a sense, Paul is commanding that we *see* each other, not just those on whom we wish to make a good impression, not just those who might benefit us in some way. Phil 2:3 is reminiscent of Rom 12:10, which makes a similar demand and which also locates it within the encompassing requirement of love: "love one another with mutual affection; outdo one another in showing honor."

It appears that Paul deliberately set out to model this behav-

---

1. Feldmeier, *Power, Service, Humility*, 65.
2. Feldmeier, *Power, Service, Humility*, 66.

ior. Only in Phil 1:1 does he describe himself by means of the single title "slave" (*doulos*).[3] As we have seen, slaves occupied the lowest social stratum, what Dio Chrysostom called "the most shameful and wretched of states."[4] Then, and in contrast to his own self-description (and only here among all of Paul's letters), he addresses recipients with the honorific titles "overseer" and "deacon."

It is all the more notable that it is only in Philippians (2:7) that Paul calls Jesus a "slave." Of course, neither Paul nor Jesus was ever literally enslaved. The point is that both humbled or "emptied" themselves (Phil 2:8), stepping down from their rightful station and willingly assuming a place among the despised. In Jesus's case, that lowering included "even death on a cross," a punishment normally reserved for slaves. It is interesting that ancient accounts of slavery often focused, not on the slaves' loss of freedom, but on their loss of honor. Likewise, accounts of crucifixion did not dwell on victims' physical suffering nearly so much as their humiliation. It was without reason that Heb 12:2 states that Jesus "endured the cross, disregarding its shame." Three centuries later, the scandal of the cross was still comprehended as it seldom is today. According to John Chrysostom, "Not every death is similar. Jesus's death seemed more disgraceful than all others; his was full of shame, his was accursed. . . . For it wasn't by killing him but by killing him in this way that they thought they would make him abominable."[5]

The contemporary analysis most relevant to our purposes is Joseph H. Hellerman's insightful *Embracing Shared Ministry: Power and Status in the Early Church and Why It Matters Today.* I have space here to highlight only a few key points of this fine book, which I warmly recommend to anyone who wishes to explore Philippians in detail.

Hellerman first describes the social situation in first-century

3. In Rom 1:1, Paul calls himself both a "slave" and "an apostle." Philippi was a distinctly Roman city, having been colonized by retired Roman soldiers. Thus, the presence of the self-designation "slave" in the greeting of these two letters (and only these two letters) is perhaps not coincidental.

4. Dio Chrysostom, *1 Serv. lib. (Or.* 14) 1.

5. Pauline Allen, *John Chrysostom: Homilies on Paul's Letter to the Philippians,* WGRW 16 (Atlanta: Society of Biblical Literature, 2013), 151–53 (Homily 8).

Philippi, making note of the importance of Roman citizenship among the city's elites. Interestingly, Philippi is the only city Luke explicitly designates a "Roman colony" (Acts 16:12), and Philippians is the only letter in which Paul employs the metaphor of "citizenship" (in 1:27 and 3:20). That Philippian citizens were keenly aware of status is evident in the hundreds of inscriptions found in the city, a large percentage of which include a detailed list of honors, for example, chiseled on a monument donated by a civic benefactor or on the tomb of a family member. Paul mimics the formula of these inscriptions in his own self-description in Phil 3:3–11, listing first honors ascribed at birth ("of the tribe of Benjamin," etc.), and then honors acquired in life ("as to the law, a Pharisee," etc.).[6] "The contents are quintessentially Jewish. The structure is transparently Roman."[7]

Paul then comments, "Yet whatever gains I had, these I have come to regard as loss because of Christ. More than that, I regard everything as loss because of the surpassing value of knowing Christ Jesus my Lord" (Phil 3:7–8a). Paul's words are evocative of Jesus's parables concerning the great cost and the still greater worth of God's reign (e.g., The Pearl of Great Price and The Treasure in the Field). Paul was fully convinced of the latter and so fully able to pay the former.

Even more striking is the "Christ hymn" of Phil 2:6–11. In verses 6–8, Paul reverses the standard formula, providing a step-by-step account of Jesus's *humiliation*.[8] Then, in verse 9, the actor changes to God, the ultimate and only true source of honor.

---

6. On ascribed and acquired honors, see Bruce J. Malina, *The New Testament World: Insights from Cultural Anthropology*, 3rd ed. (Louisville, KY: Westminster John Knox, 2001), 32–36.

7. Hellerman, *Embracing Shared Ministry*, 131.

8. Compare 2 Cor 8:9: "For you know the generous act of our Lord Jesus Christ, that though he was rich, yet for your sakes he became poor, so that by his poverty you might become rich." Writes Linda L. Belleville, "By 'rich' (*plousios*) Paul is probably thinking of the riches of heavenly existence. . . . By 'he became poor' (*eptōcheusen)* he undoubtedly has in mind the incarnation" ("'Imitate Me, Just as I Imitate Christ': 1–2 Corinthians," in *Patterns of Discipleship in the New Testament*, ed. Richard N. Longenecker [Grand Rapids: Eerdmans, 1996], 128).

Jesus "humbled himself," but God has "exalted him" to the highest place, with the name "above every name." He, not Caesar, is "Lord" (v. 11).

In his *The New Testament World,* Bruce Malina observed that "Honor is always presumed to exist within one's own family of blood. . . . It is with all these others that one must play the game, engage in the contest, put one's honor and one's own family honor on the line."[9] Hellerman builds on this observation by noting how Paul's repeated use of familial language—describing fellow believers as "brothers" and "sisters," and God as "Father"—undermines the quest for individual honor.[10] Siblings were expected to rejoice in and to benefit from each other's successes and not to compete with one another for glory. While acknowledging rivalries and the injustices siblings sometimes inflicted on each other, Plutarch, a contemporary of Paul, advised his readers,

> [I]n the first place, to make his brothers partners in those respects in which he is considered to be superior, adorning them with a portion of his repute and adopting them into his friendships, and if he is a cleverer speaker than they, to make his eloquence available for their use as though it were no less theirs than his; in the next place, to make manifest to them neither haughtiness nor disdain, but rather, by deferring to them and conforming his character to theirs, to make his superiority secure from envy and to equalize, so far as this is attainable, the disparity of his fortune by his moderation of spirit.[11]

This comes remarkably close to Paul's own admonition to the Philippians. Hellerman concludes,

9. Malina, *New Testament World,* 36.
10. "The sibling metaphor is Paul's most frequent way of speaking of his fellow Christ-followers, and almost his only way of addressing them directly." Cf. William S. Campbell, *Paul and the Creation of Christian Identity* (New York: T&T Clark, 2008), 36. On the occasional use of familial language by other Greco-Roman groups (associations), see Philip A. Harland, *Dynamics of Identity in the World of the Early Christians* (London: Continuum, 2009), 63–96.
11. Plutarch, *Frat. amor.* (*On Brotherly Love*) 484D (Helmbold, LCL).

Paul's strategy was truly brilliant. He recognized that only in the social context of a healthy surrogate family ... could Jesus's ideal of servant leadership triumph over the social values of the dominant culture and become a reality among the Philippian Christians.[12]

Talk about family values.

Galatians

The most troubled of Paul's churches was located in Galatia, in present-day Turkey. While the crisis at Galatia was overtly theological, concerning the question of whether Gentile Christians must obey some or perhaps all of the Jewish law, it is apparent that status also played a role in the controversy. Paul's opponents challenged his authority, telling the Galatians that he was at best a second-rate apostle. Worse still, they claimed that he had sold them Gospel-lite, a watered-down version of Christianity served up for easy conversions (Gal 1:10). In short, they were the superior missionaries, and superior believers naturally should follow them. In 6:13, Paul states that the new arrivals "want you to be circumcised so that they may boast about your flesh," that is, that they might brag about their successes converting Paul's Gentile believers to full(er) Jewish practice. Here, as in Philippians, Paul argues that the actual motive behind the controversy is standard-issue self-promotion. Of course, we have only Paul's side of the story; nonetheless, these are words in season for the church today. His next sentence summarizes his perspective and could just as easily have been written to the Corinthians: "May I never boast except in the cross of our Lord Jesus Christ, through which the world has been crucified to me, and I to the world" (Gal 6:14). Paul did not hate the world. He did realize, however, that identifying with one whom the world crucified meant putting to death the expectation of that same world's approval.

12. Hellerman, *Embracing Shared Ministry*, 198.

Another interesting point about Galatians: the majority of the "works of the flesh" listed in chapter 5 are not personal or even explicitly religious in nature. They are social. Just after "idolatry and sorcery" come "enmities, strife, jealousy, anger, quarrels, dissensions, factions [and] envy." (Gal 5:20–21a). These are the most numerous among the "passions and desires" of the flesh that "those who belong to Christ have crucified" (Gal 5:24).

Paul locates these various forms of rivalry in "the flesh," that is, imbedded in human nature. They are not temptations from without but from within. So it is no good watching over the walls when the enemy is already resident within the gates. As before, Paul finds the answer in the cross. On one level, he sees the crucifixion as the ultimate expression of Jesus's self-emptying love. Jesus is the example for believers who also deny themselves, endure the world's rejection, and look to God to, in a sense, "give them a name" (Phil 2:9). On a more profound and mysterious level, Paul believes that those who belong to Christ participate both in his crucifixion and his resurrection (Phil 2:19–20). The former is not simply a means by which sins are forgiven. Those parts of our human nature that war against others and against God were in Jesus nailed to the cross. The Spirit then enables believers to live a new quality, a resurrection quality, of life. Admittedly, participation in Christ is not among Paul's more comprehensible ideas, but it is nevertheless central to his thought.

Paul goes on to list the contrasting "fruits of the Spirit," and it follows that most, two-thirds in fact, are social virtues: love (first, of course), peace, patience, kindness, generosity, and gentleness. Paul's choice of words is deliberate. These are not "works" resulting from the disposition or efforts of the individual—a result, in other words, in which one might boast. Instead, they are fruits nurtured by the Spirit. This parallels Paul's discussion of spiritual gifts in 1 Cor 12 and Rom 12: "To each is given the manifestation of the Spirit for the common good" (1 Cor 12:7). In Galatians, the passage concludes:

> If we live by the Spirit, let us also be guided by the Spirit. Let us not become conceited, competing against one another, envying one another. (Gal 5:25–26)

As we had said before, one cannot be both full of oneself and filled by the Spirit. It is no accident that a letter seeking to resolve a theological dispute would take this turn. However theoretical in content, disagreements occur amongst humans, for whom self-interest is a primary motive.

Consider for a moment the close relationship between theological novelty and status. Max Weber, the great sociologist, stated that authority was often granted in religion on the basis of perceived proximity to the sacred.[13] In Christianity, the sacred, God, is most proximate in the person of Jesus, and next in those individuals closest to Him. For that reason, Jesus's original disciples had less trouble exercising authority than Paul, however diligently he might labor and however heroically he might suffer. Likewise, those who claim to know more of or to have special insight into Jesus's teaching will be regarded as possessing special authority by those who accept their impressive sounding assertions.

This is the particular bane of Protestantism, which credits the Bible with unique proximity to the sacred as "the Word of God" but which thereby unintentionally encourages increasingly esoteric and idiosyncratic scriptural interpretations. If the Bible is authoritative but you have to go to Rev. John Doe to understand it, then Rev. Doe shares in Scripture's authority, much as the moon reflects and shares the sun's radiance. To the extent that Rev. Doe's teachings cannot be heard elsewhere and yet seem credible, his authority increases proportionately. When Rev. Doe's unique insights are thought to be indispensable to salvation, his authority becomes nearly absolute.

I watched this dynamic unfold within an independent Christian group many years ago. The co-pastors, a married couple, began their ministry conventionally enough. Over a period of years, however, they introduced increasingly idiosyncratic teaching from

13. See the discussion of charismatic authority in Max Weber, *Economy and Society: An Outline of Interpretive Sociology,* trans. Ephraim Fischoff (New York: Bedminster, 1968), 241–54. A helpful evaluation and application of Weber's theories is provided in Bengt Holmberg, *Paul and Power: The Structure of Authority in the Primitive Church as Reflected in the Pauline Epistles* (Philadelphia: Fortress, 1978), 137–60.

the pulpit, not least about themselves. Ultimately, they led the congregation into a sectarian and, by even a charitable appraisal, unorthodox theology. The leaders seemed to crave attention and to have landed upon a strategy for getting it: become privileged dispensers of essential knowledge. For their part, the congregation appeared to act as enablers. They benefitted from their close association with these spiritual giants, and in time they came to regard their very distinctive form of Christianity as the only legitimate brand. Hence, the honor they showered on their leaders redounded to their own glory.

That group taught me something about the relationship between theology, status, and authority. The thousands of divisions within the church, especially within Protestantism, now appeared less surprising. Of course, the world is a complicated place, and every schism cannot be reduced to a clash of egos. But surely, many can be. Moreover, our willingness to identify with a faction is in no small part due to our desire to be seen to be in the right, to justify ourselves, leading us to overestimate our purity, overstate our knowledge, and overrate our importance.

The desire for status is thus a dynamic engine of heresy. Esoteric knowledge, such as one finds in ancient Gnostic circles and modern secret societies, is alluring. "The Old, Old Story" can look awfully drab in the presence of such gaudy competitors. Much the same dynamic is at work in present-day fascination with conspiracy theories. Scarcely a month passes without another book or television show purporting to reveal the Bible's heretofore "hidden secrets" or "mysteries." Insider information is seductive. Its possession makes one special, and in the Internet age, anyone with sufficient cleverness, time, and disregard for the rules of evidence can find an enabling audience. Not that the world has changed all that much. 1 Tim 6:3–5 speaks of "conceited" leaders who are guided by

> A morbid craving for controversy and for disputes about words. From these come envy, dissension, slander, base suspicions, and wrangling among those who are depraved in mind and bereft of the truth, imagining that godliness is a means of gain.

So, Paul may well have been right to claim that some preached Christ out of "selfish ambition" and that a theological difference was actually motivated by a desire to boast. Moreover, the willingness of some converts in both Galatia and Corinth to endure more demanding teachers might have been attributable to their desire to be part of a more elite group of believers. If so, these were neither the first nor the last to seek earthly glory by means of heavenly things.

James

We turn now to three other New Testament letters: James, 1 Peter, and 1 John. The precise dating, authorship, and audience of these epistles are subjects of irresolvable scholarly dispute, but that need not concern us. What matters is that these letters provide additional examples of leaders attempting to conform early church communities to the pattern of Christ.

James is a book of practical wisdom, distant kin to the Old Testament book of Proverbs. Unlike Hebrews or Paul's epistles to the Romans and to the Galatians, it does not contain a sustained argument. Instead, it is more like the discourses of Jesus. Indeed, there are several parallels between James and the Gospels. For example, the command to pray without doubting (Jas 1:5–6) resembles Matt 7:7–8; the prohibition of oaths (Jas 5:12) recalls Matt 5:34–37; Jas 2:8, "Love your neighbor as yourself," brings to mind Jesus's own quotations of Lev 19:18; and the warning to rich oppressors (Jas 5:1–2) sounds a lot like Luke 6:24.

As a consequence of the Protestant Reformation, the epistle of James is known mostly for its (to Martin Luther, problematic) account of the relationship between faith and works. This is a good illustration of the way systematic theology overshadows, even crowds out, practical theology. In point of fact, the greater part of the letter is devoted to the task of helping its readers to get along with each other. The problems James identifies and the solutions he proposes will be immediately recognizable to readers of this book.

The first chapter of James highlights matters to be treated in more detail elsewhere in the letter. Near the top of the list is the issue of status, specifically, one's perception of the poor and the rich:

> Let the believer who is lowly boast in being raised up, and the rich in being brought low, because the rich will disappear like a flower in the field. For the sun rises with its scorching heat and withers the field; its flower falls, and its beauty perishes. It is the same way with the rich; in the midst of a busy life, they will wither away. (1:9–11)

We recall Matt 6:28–30, Jesus's teaching about the transitory "lilies of the field." The metaphor here is the same, but the meaning is somewhat different. In Matthew, the lesson concerned trusting God for provision: "But if God so clothes the grass of the field, which is alive today and tomorrow is thrown into the oven, will he not much more clothe you—you of little faith? (Matt 6:30; see also Isa 40:6–9). The link between the two passages is provided by Matthew's mention of Solomon, the wealthiest king of Israel: "even Solomon in all his glory was not clothed like one of these" (Matt 6:29). Little remained of Solomon's glory in the first century, most remnants of which had been destroyed half a millennium before under the "scorching heat" of the Babylonian conquest.

This is a classic example of reconceptualization. The poor are "raised up" both in the present, through their new status in Christ, and in the future, at the resurrection, when such earthly distinctions will perish and when present-day faithfulness will be rewarded. By contrast, rich believers are brought low both in the present, since they much acknowledge their equal need before God, and in the future, since any material advantage they now enjoy will be forfeit.

The subject is taken up in more detail at the beginning of the next chapter:

> My brothers and sisters, do you with your acts of favoritism really believe in our glorious Lord Jesus Christ? For if a person with gold rings and in fine clothes comes into your assembly,

and if a poor person in dirty clothes also comes in, and if you take notice of the one wearing the fine clothes and say, "Have a seat here, please," while to the one who is poor you say, "Stand there," or, "Sit at my feet," have you not made distinctions among yourselves, and become judges with evil thoughts? (Jas 2:1–4)

The diametrical contrast between believing in Jesus and making distinctions amongst people is striking. It reminds us of Paul's statement in 2 Cor 5:16: "we regard no one from a human point of view; even though we once knew Christ from a human point of view, we know him no longer in that way." To believe that the crucified Christ is "glorious" is to buy into a way of seeing the world in which conventional human attributions of glory cannot hold. What is more, Jesus's own behavior toward the marginalized makes such distinctions indefensible.

To glorify the rich and despise the poor is to "become judges with evil thoughts." It is the vocation of judges to make distinctions between people, in particular, to divide the guilty from the innocent. An evil judge is one who cannot act disinterestedly because he or she has a personal stake in the verdict. We, too, have something at stake when we distinguish amongst people for the sake of personal advantage, whether social or financial. It is a species of bribery, and it prevents us from acting justly. "If you show partiality, you commit sin and are convicted by the law as trangressors" (Jas 2:9).

Such conduct "dishonors the poor" (Jas 2:6). That the poor deserve honor is assumed. In fact, the poor have a special, even a preferred, place: "Has not God chosen the poor in the world to be rich in faith and to be heirs of the kingdom that he has promised to those who love him?" (Jas 2:5). By contrast, the rich are those who most often oppress and scorn believers (Jas 2:6–7). By what logic does it make sense to favor such persons?

Love is once more cited as the decisive consideration: "You do well if you really fulfill the royal law according to the scripture, 'You shall love your neighbor as yourself.'" (Jas 2:8, quoting Lev 19:18). We are again reminded of a passage in the Gospels, in this case, Luke 10:29: "But wanting to justify himself, he asked Jesus,

'And who is my neighbor?'" In Luke it is the Samaritan who proves the true neighbor. The commandment has much the same force here. The neighbor includes the apparent outsider, the one you would not expect to assist you.

James also has a good bit to say on the subject of wisdom. Again, the topic is highlighted in the first chapter: "If any of you is lacking in wisdom, ask God, who gives to all generously and ungrudgingly, and it will be given you" (Jas 1:5). This verse is often quoted as persons recount moments when they petitioned God for insight. There is nothing wrong with that practice; nevertheless, it is interesting to see that when James returns to the subject, he has in mind a quite specific kind of wisdom:

> Who is wise and understanding among you? Show by your good life that your works are done with gentleness born of wisdom. But if you have bitter envy and selfish ambition in your hearts, do not be boastful and false to the truth. Such wisdom does not come down from above, but is earthly, unspiritual, devilish. For where there is envy and selfish ambition, there will also be disorder and wickedness of every kind. But the wisdom from above is first pure, then peaceable, gentle, willing to yield, full of mercy and good fruits, without a trace of partiality or hypocrisy. And a harvest of righteousness is sown in peace for those who make peace. (Jas 3:13–18)

One could hardly ask for a better summary of New Testament teaching on this subject. It is earthly, unspiritual, even "devilish" to be boastful, envious, selfish and partial. Such a mindset leaves disorder and "wickedness of every kind" in its wake. To be wise is to have the perspective of heaven, by which the community is equipped to live in peace, "full of mercy and good fruits." It is also to be "true to the truth," which for Christians means living according to the remarkable example of Jesus, "without a trace of partiality or hypocrisy."

Rhetorically, James treats wisdom much the way Paul treats spiritual gifts. The Corinthians employed gifts of the Spirit as status markers. Paul argued that the greatest gift, love, is the one that empowers people to live together harmoniously, heedless of distinctions. Likewise, true wisdom does not elevate some above others. To the contrary, to be wise is to be humble.

James's discussion of wisdom follows immediately on the heels of a short essay about the destructive power of "the tongue." "How great a forest is set ablaze by a small fire! And the tongue is a fire" (Jas 3:5b-6a). James might have railed against swearing, against using the Lord's name in vain, against pronouncing false oaths, or other such sins of speech. Instead, the concern is once again social in nature: "With it [the tongue] we bless the Lord and Father, and with it we curse those who are made in the likeness of God" (Jas 3:9). Why denigrate others? More often than not, it is to elevate ourselves.

James devotes the entire next chapter to a discussion of quarrelling, judging, and boasting, expanding upon his earlier comments. A single verse may serve as summary: "Humble yourselves before the Lord, and he will exalt you" (Jas 4:10). As we have seen so many times before, this coin has two sides. The goal is not self-abnegation, the loss of identity. But something must be lost if something greater is to be gained. To find one's meaning in God, one must recognize one's need of God for meaning.

1 Peter

First Peter was written from Rome to a group of predominantly if not exclusively Gentile churches in Asia Minor. The letter's chief goal is to offer encouragement to those suffering mistreatment for their faith. That is the context of the passage already quoted in chapter 2:

> For to this you have been called, because Christ also suffered for you, leaving you an example, so that you should follow in his steps. "He committed no sin, and no deceit was found in his mouth." When he was abused, he did not return abuse; when he suffered, he did not threaten; but he entrusted himself to the one who judges justly. (1 Pet 2:21–23)

Jesus could do what he did because "he entrusted himself" to God's judgment. Here, as elsewhere, readers are advised to take a heavenly view of their earthly experience (e.g., 1 Pet 1:3–4, 13–14, 21). Although facing disapproval now, they may anticipate a future in which their sacrifices are rewarded:

> In this you rejoice, though now for a little while you may have to suffer various trials, so that the genuineness of your faith, more precious than gold which though perishable is tested by fire, may redound to praise and glory and honor at the revelation of Jesus Christ. (1 Pet 1:6–7; see also 1:4–5)

First Peter 4:4 is a close parallel: "when the chief shepherd appears, you will win the crown of glory that never fades away." Paul offers the same contrast in 1 Cor 9:25: "Athletes exercise self-control in all things; they do it to receive a perishable wreath, but we an imperishable one." The reference is to a wreath made of branches and leaves, often of the bay laurel plant, which crowned the winners of athletic contests such as the Olympics. Wreaths were also worn by victorious Roman military commanders. They were thus a highly prized status symbol, a "crown of [earthly] glory." Like a prom corsage, however, they were destined to fade. It is sobering to recall that Jesus was instead crowned by Rome with thorns. The audience of this letter had not likely suffered to that degree, but they had experienced public humiliation because of their faith (1 Pet 4:4), and the promise of future vindication recurs throughout the letter.

As we would expect, the author intends that this heavenly perspective should influence relationships of readers with one another:

> Finally, all of you, have unity of spirit, sympathy, love for one another, a tender heart, and a humble mind. Do not repay evil for evil or abuse for abuse; but, on the contrary, repay with a blessing. It is for this that you were called—that you might inherit a blessing. For "Those who desire life and desire to see good days, let them keep their tongues from evil and their lips from

speaking deceit; let them turn away from evil and do good; let them seek peace and pursue it." (1 Pet 3:8–11, citing Ps 34:12–16)

This passage recalls many of the themes we encountered in James, including the proper use of the tongue (Jas 3:1–12) and the desirability of unity and peace (Jas 3:18). Both James and 1 Peter go on to quote Prov 3:34:

And all of you must clothe yourselves with humility in your dealings with one another, for "God opposes the proud, but gives grace to the humble." (1 Pet 5:5b = Jas 4:6)

And both offer a nearly identical summary command:

Humble yourselves before the Lord, and he will exalt you. (Jas 4:10)

Humble yourselves therefore under the mighty hand of God, so that he may exalt you in due time. (1 Pet 5:6)

Most significantly, both regard love as the supreme standard of Christian conduct: "Above all, maintain constant love for one another, for love covers a multitude of sins" (1 Pet 4:8). I came to appreciate this verse after I became a parent. Parents know many if not all of the faults and failings of their children. Love does not overlook them; instead, it "covers" them. The Greek verb used here, *kaluptein*, is the root of "apocalypse": an "uncovering" or "revelation." Love is by contrast unrevealing, engaged neither in private reminder nor public exposure. Love does not keep score, in other words. It makes relationships out of what would otherwise be serial transactions.

This phase, "covers a multitude of sins," is probably borrowed from Prov 10:12b and appears in the final verse of James (5:20). It is also in the late first-century letter 1 Clement (49:5; also 2 Clem 15:4), which, interestingly enough, was written to the congregation Paul founded a generation earlier at Corinth. This suggests that it was a common Christian teaching. The recurrence of the love commandment, going back to Jesus himself, hardly needs stressing. In Paul's own correspondence with the Corinthian Christians, love is listed as chief amongst God's gifts. It is interesting that 1 Peter's mention of love is followed immediately by a discussion of gifts:

> Be hospitable to one another without complaining. Like good stewards of the manifold grace of God, serve one another with whatever gift each of you has received. Whoever speaks must do so as one speaking the very words of God; whoever serves must do so with the strength that God supplies, so that God may be glorified in all things through Jesus Christ. To him belong the glory and the power forever and ever. Amen. (1 Pet 4:9–11)

As in 1 Corinthians, gifts are given that believers might effectively serve one another. They are stewards, not possessors, of such gifts, which are given to "each," not to a saintly few. Ultimately, their use brings glory to God.

Finally, like James (1:11), Matthew (6:30), and Luke (12:28), 1 Peter employs the metaphor of the grass of the field, in this case quoting Isa 40:6–9 directly:

> "All flesh is like grass and all its glory like the flower of grass. The grass withers, and the flower falls, but the word of the Lord abides forever." That word is the good news which was preached to you. (1 Pet 1:24–25)

This follows upon the command to "love one another deeply from the heart" (1 Pet 1:22b). The author of 1 Peter was acutely conscious of life's transitory nature. Such awareness removes many barriers to love. One not engaged in building a shrine to oneself is more free to see and respond to the needs of others. "You can't take it with you" applies to reputations as well as to possessions.

Texts such as those quoted from 1 Peter above might by now seem repetitious, and it is for that reason that this brief tour will make only one more stop. Still, it is important to note such consistency. I am cautious about speaking of *the* New Testament perspective on a given subject. The distinctive voices of its authors are too often muted by generalization. The present study pushes in the opposite direction, however. What seems most noteworthy is the conspicuous commonality. This indicates that certain problems were widespread, that they were thought significant enough to address, and that those who addressed them drew from a shared well of theological understanding. Hopefully, recognizing these facts will encourage us to take these matters seriously ourselves. What was once scandalous may seem normal with the passage of time. Distinctions and divisions within the church ought never to become ordinary.

1 John

The community for which 1 John was composed had experienced just such a division. First John 2:19 refers to some persons who "went out from us, but they did not belong to us; for if they had belonged to us, they would have remained with us. But by going out they made it plain that none of them belongs to us." At least in part, the conflict appears to have arisen over differing views of Jesus, specifically, of his full humanity: "By this you know the Spirit of God: every spirit that confesses that Jesus Christ has come in the flesh is from God" (1 John 4:2). This statement is closely paralleled by 2 John 7:

> Many deceivers have gone out into the world, those who do not confess that Jesus Christ has come in the flesh; any such person is the deceiver and the antichrist!

Most scholars think these verses refer to an early form of Docetism, the belief that Jesus only *seemed* (from the verb *dokeō*) to be human. That would explain the emphasis upon physicality in 1 John 1:1 ("what we have looked at and touched with our own hands") and the insistence in 1 John 5:6 that Jesus came "not with the water only but with the water and the blood." It appears at least that

Jesus's humanity was greatly depreciated if not entirely denied by those who had left the Johannine community.

Body/spirit dualism was common in the ancient world, just as it is common in some circles today. Many regarded the body as an encumbrance or trap from which the right sort of religion would free them. Some went so far as to regard materiality as a curse imposed upon humanity by an evil deity. Naturally, such a viewpoint was at odds with the belief God had created the physical universe and pronounced it good. For that reason, second-century Christians of a strongly dualistic persuasion had difficulty retaining the Old Testament as Scripture. They also had trouble with the doctrine of the incarnation. One example is the Gnostic Basilides, who, according to Irenaeus, taught that:

> "[T]he father . . . sent his own first-begotten Nous [Mind] (he it is who is called Christ) to bestow deliverance on them that believe in him, from the power of those who made the world. He appeared, then, on earth as a man. . . . Wherefore he did not himself suffer death, but Simon . . . being compelled, bore the cross in his stead; so that this latter being transfigured by him, that he might be thought to be Jesus, was crucified . . . while Jesus himself received the form of Simon, and, standing by, laughed at them. . . . Those, then, who know these things have been freed from the principalities who formed the world; so that it is not incumbent on us to confess him who was crucified, but him who came in the form of a man. . . . If anyone, therefore . . . confesses the crucified, that man is still a slave, and under the power of those who formed our bodies; but he who denies him has been freed from these beings."[14]

Fascinating as this is, why mention this controversy in a chapter about status? The controversy compels us to consider the issue of otherworldliness. All of this talk about the reality of the reign of God, of having a heavenly perspective, of being aware of the transitory nature of life (fields of grass and all that) raises serious

14. Irenaeus, *Haer.* (*Against Heresies*) 24.4.

questions. Are we simply to check out of this world in expectation of the next? Is it true after all that Christians are too heavenly minded to be of any earthly good? Should locating our identity in God cause us to abandon the expectation of doing meaningful work here and now?

The seeds of discord that had come into bloom by the time of 1 John may have been sown in the Gospel of John itself. (I assume that 1 John was written after the Gospel and to a Johannine community.) The Gospel of John is significantly though not thoroughly dualistic. Persons are either in the light or in darkness (John 12:46); children of God or children of the devil (John 8:42–44); born of the flesh or (re)born of the Spirit (John 3:6). The humanity of Jesus is evident—"the Word became flesh" (John 1:14a) and actually died on a cross (John 19:30)—but the Gospel focuses overwhelmingly upon Jesus's divinity. It is not hard to see how a group of Johannine Christians might have come gradually to jettison the idea of incarnation, enfleshment, entirely in favor of a purely divine, spiritual Jesus, especially if their goal was to become pure spirit themselves.

In short, they fell prey to the very temptation we ourselves must withstand, that of polarizing God and creation. It is no accident that heretical systems of the sort described above typically offered an alternative creation myth in which the physical order was shown to be a mistake. Materiality was thus the problem that religion solved. While few Christians today would go quite that far, less extreme forms of otherworldliness are still to be found. Unhealthy religion is often escapist religion, absolving adherents of responsibility for the state of the world around them.

First John draws a line in the sand, but it must be said that the book inhabits a world located just this side of that line. For example:

> Do not love the world or the things in the world. The love of the Father is not in those who love the world; for all that is in the world—the desire of the flesh, the desire of the eyes, the pride in riches—comes not from the Father but from the world. And the world and its desire are passing away, but those who do the will of God live forever. (1 John 2:15–17; compare John 15:18.)

Here, "the world" is not so much the physical creation as it is the present world order. Specifically and directly relevant to this study, it is the world of unchecked desire and unbridled pride that is at variance with the will of God. The threefold description is traditional and goes back to the temptation story in the Garden of Eden in Gen 3:6:

> So when the woman saw that the tree was good for food, and that it was a delight to the eyes, and that the tree was to be desired to make one wise, she took of its fruit and ate; and she also gave some to her husband, who was with her, and he ate.

The goodness of creation was thus thwarted by human craving. In themselves, there is nothing wrong with food, beauty, or wisdom. All were already abundantly present. As C. S. Lewis said, the devil is a spoiler, not a creator, of pleasure.[15] When enough good is no longer good enough, the appropriate goal becomes the controlling obsession.

Several New Testament books appear to have been written in the context of actual or threatening persecution, Revelation being the preeminent example. We have already included on that list both Mark and 1 Peter. The Gospel of John was likely written to a Christian community that had recently been sundered from Judaism. (In John, the opposition of "the Jews" is mentioned repeatedly, and Jesus explicitly warns his followers that they will be "put out of the synagogue;" see John 9:22 and 12:42). We also should bear in mind that we are considering a historical period dominated by the Roman Empire, void of democratic election, minority rights, and popular reform. Add to that a short life expectancy due to unsanitary conditions and untreatable disease. In that context, many contemporary philosophical schools taught that the best way to deal with the world, abrim with inequities and hazards, was to learn to live with it. Be happy where you are with what you have because the big wide world is not going to change.

---

15. C. S. Lewis, *The Screwtape Letters* (New York: Macmillan, 1962), 41–42. The demon Screwtape writes that his aim is to create in humans "an ever increasing craving for an ever diminishing pleasure" (42).

It is wholly understandable that those enmeshed in such a bleak situation would view the earth as an inhospitable place. That is not the space most of us inhabit today, at least not to the same extent. In particular, we are free and responsible agents to a degree that few ancients could have imagined. That means we have both opportunities and obligations the everyday Hittite or Roman did not.

For the sake of focus and manageability, this study is restricted to the New Testament, but that helpful limit is also an unhelpful limitation. Most if not all of the New Testament authors read the Old Testament as Scripture, and our view of the world likewise needs to be informed by that broader perspective. Most vital is a proper doctrine of creation, which sees the physical cosmos as something inherently good and our world as a place where God is active. God does not meet and ennoble only kings and priests, but also shepherds, vinedressers, judges, administrators, counselors, carpenters, scribes, goldsmiths, textile workers, merchants, laundry workers, musicians, and potters.

The biblical view of the world is balanced, in other words. To find one's meaning first and foremost in God does not require that we find nothing meaningful on Earth. Indeed, it is God alone who can give lasting meaning to earthly endeavor. The paradigm is once again Jesus, who, fully convinced of the reality of God's dominion, ate with lepers, healed the sick, and washed disciples' feet. It does not get any more this-worldly than that.

In addition, 1 John addresses the practical side of theological controversy. As we would expect in such a context, the word "know" occurs repeatedly throughout the letter,[16] as does "true/truth/truly."[17] Obviously, the author cares that his readers know the truth. What we might not anticipate is the number of verses on the subject of love. Indeed, to quote them all would be to reproduce a substantial part of the book.

The connection between knowing the truth and acting in love is made explicit in 1 John 2:

16. 1 John 2:3, 4, 11, 13, 14, 18, 20, 21, 29; 3:1, 2, 5, 6, 14, 15, 16, 19, 20, etc.
17. 1 John 1:3, 6, 8; 2:4, 5, 8, 21, 27; 3:18, 19; 4:6; 5:6, 20.

Now by this we may be sure that we know him, if we obey his commandments. Whoever says, "I have come to know him," but does not obey his commandments, is a liar, and in such a person the truth does not exist; but whoever obeys his word, truly in this person the love of God has reached perfection. By this we may be sure that we are in him: whoever says, "I abide in him," ought to walk just as he walked. (1 John 2:3–6)

In John 13:34, Jesus says, "I give you a new commandment, that you love one another. Just as I have loved you, you also should love one another." First John 2:7–11 refers to this commandment and employs it as a standard for judging between true and false believers: "But whoever hates another believer is in the darkness, walks in the darkness, and does not know the way to go, because the darkness has brought on blindness" (1 John 2:11). In other words, John faults the schismatics not only with wrong belief but with failure to love. Had they loved their fellow believers, they would not deliberately have split the church.

The children of God and the children of the devil are revealed in this way: all who do not do what is right are not from God, nor are those who do not love their brothers and sisters. For this is the message you have heard from the beginning, that we should love one another. We must not be like Cain who was from the evil one and murdered his brother. And why did he murder him? Because his own deeds were evil and his brother's righteous. (1 John 3:10–12)

Cain kills out of jealousy. The attitude he evinces in Gen 4:9 is precisely the opposite of love: "Then the Lord said to Cain, 'Where is your brother Abel?' He said, 'I do not know; am I my brother's keeper?'" The same point is made in 1 John 4:19–21:

We love because he first loved us. Those who say, "I love God," and hate their brothers or sisters, are liars; for those who do not love a brother or sister whom they have seen, cannot love God whom they have not seen. The commandment we have from him is this: those who love God must love their brothers and sisters also.

We cannot be certain in detail of the background to this letter—what persons led the walkout, what they themselves thought and, especially, what motivated them. We do know however that 1 John steadfastly associates their wrong beliefs with a deficit of love. Perhaps like Cain, their contention was born of envy.

Permit me to quote one final passage, entirely out of admiration. A look at 1 John would be incomplete without citing 4:7–12:

> Beloved, let us love one another, because love is from God; everyone who loves is born of God and knows God. Whoever does not love does not know God, for God is love. God's love was revealed among us in this way: God sent his only Son into the world so that we might live through him. In this is love, not that we loved God but that he loved us and sent his Son to be the atoning sacrifice for our sins. Beloved, since God loved us so much, we also ought to love one another. No one has ever seen God; if we love one another, God lives in us, and his love is perfected in us.

As we have seen, New Testament authors repeatedly deal with the issue of church conflict, especially conflict over status, by enjoining believers to love. Characteristically, we are told to love because we ourselves already are loved. God's love for us is reflected and perfected in our love for others. No one who knew that love deeply would worry about status. Anyone who truly knows that love is set free to serve joyfully in this world.

The Real Thing

Experienced bank tellers are so accustomed to handling money that they may know by touch that a bill is a forgery. Similarly, readers of this book should by now have gained a feel for authentic Christian teaching on matters related to social status. No teller handles every bill in circulation; neither have we reviewed every relevant New Testament passage. Even less have we attempted to document all forms of counterfeit spirituality. Still, we have handled enough texts with sufficient care that we should be equipped to distinguish more readily between teaching that is genuinely and spuriously Christian.

CHAPTER EIGHT

Ambition

Intelligence without ambition is a bird without wings.
SALVADOR DALI

"Eva, beware your ambition. It's hungry and cold, can't be controlled, will run wild."
AUGUSTINE MAGALDI
(AS PORTRAYED IN EVITA)

The juxtaposition of the above two quotations illustrates the problem we shall consider in this chapter. The first is a favorite of motivational speakers seeking to stir up ambition in their audiences, encouraging the expectation that greater diligence and more single-minded determination will yield surpassing success. For their part, moralists can sound like Magaldi as depicted in the Tim Rice and Andrew Lloyd Weber musical *Evita*, warning of the ruinous dangers of ambition, of its benign face and ruthless heart.

Both are right to a point. There are opposing sides to this thing we call ambition, one productive and one destructive. It is a slippery word precisely because of its many, varied, and contradictory associations. So, how are we to define—much less to think theologically about—ambition?

We might begin by describing ambition as a strong inner drive directed toward a specific goal. It can be encouraged from without, but it is not coerced. It has an aim, some desirable object or state of being. As Brian J. Mahan put it, "There is no such thing as ambition in general. Desire in its raw specificity is always *for* this or that."[1]

Survival and procreation would qualify by this definition, but they are not normally categorized as ambitions. Ordinarily, what we call ambitions attempt to satisfy abstract perceived needs, such as security, luxury or, especially, status. Survival and procreation are concrete and binary; either you do or you do not live or have offspring. On the other hand, one's sense of security or status resides on a sliding scale, and one could in theory exist without either. Moreover, the form in which an ambition is satisfied is culturally (and to an extent individually) determined. What conveys status in one society might carry no meaning in another. I could wear a laurel wreath to work tomorrow, but it would not impress, at least not in a way I might like.

This is an admittedly imperfect characterization, but it can at least serve as a starting point for our discussion. My chief concern is to acknowledge the complexity of the concept, to recognize that "ambition" covers a veritable waterfront of human behavior, some of which is bad and some good. The essential thing is to learn to distinguish between the two.

The degree to which one is ambitious is at least partly a function of one's physiology. Not surprisingly, ambition correlates to some extent with extroversion. Persons who are extroverted are more responsive to the brain chemical dopamine, which results in "a high degree of activity in a network of structures in the brain— often called the 'reward system'—including the orbitofrontal cortex, the nucleus accumbens, and the amygdala."[2] Thus, extroverts more than introverts "are characterized by their tendency to seek rewards, from top dog status to sexual highs to cold cash. They've been found to have greater economic, political, and hedo-

---

1. Mahan, *Forgetting Ourselves on Purpose*, 90.
2. Cain, *Quiet*, 160.

nistic ambitions than introverts."[3] Highly ambitious persons may therefore engage in risky or even unethical behavior that the more temperate would shun. On the other hand, to possess no motivation, no desire, no passion, no interest, no drive, no enthusiasm is indeed to be like a bird without wings or, more familiarly, to be a bump on a log or a wet rag.

We might wish to judge an ambition based upon its source, but such knowledge is elusive. Each of us is an extraordinarily complex product of both nature and nurture, and we are not always good judges of our own motives. Alternatively, ambitions may be assessed by their goal and degree. Ambition for what and at what cost?

My experience with pastors and other Christian leaders encourages me to consider the matter more fully. What follows is therefore an exploration, nearly a meditation, on the subject. My hope is that it will stimulate reflection and, especially, more open discussion of the topic within the church.

I mention pastors because they are in an especially conflicted position. It takes a certain amount of ambition to jump through the many hoops required to enter ordained ministry, which for many includes completing a three-year master's degree. It takes an even higher level of ambition to tackle with energy, eagerness, and imagination a long-term appointment at a church. I cannot imagine a fruitful pastor who is not ambitious, who does not dream dreams, see visions, and then work vigorously toward their realization. God is not laissez-faire, and faithful ministry is active ministry.

Vocation and Career

Were that all there is to it, ministers would have no reason to kid themselves or anyone else about their ambition, would have no need to master the art of being—without actually appearing to be—ambitious. "Of course I am ambitious. I am a pastor!" In

3. Cain, *Quiet*, 159.

reality, most persons I know in professional ministry are ambivalent about their own ambition, and rightly so. To enter ministry is to choose a life of service. It is to assume a vocation as participant in the work of Jesus. To admit to ambition is to open oneself to the charge of putting fame or wealth or some other object, some other idol, in the place of God. So "ambition" is an uncomfortable word for those in ministry, ambitious though they might be.

My own career as a pastor and a professor is neither a triumph nor a tragedy. It is instead a mixture of achievement and disappointment, of wins and losses, of ambitions realized and thwarted. Some things have gone better than I had reason to expect, but others worse. I have been both unfairly advantaged and, more rarely, disadvantaged. In short, my story is rather typical and so broadly correlates with the experience of most pastors and other so-called professionals.

The choice of the word "career" is deliberate. Except on the most general level, the New Testament has almost nothing to say about careers, even careers in ministry. It does however talk quite a bit about living one's life within the framework of a calling or, to use our preferred term, a vocation (from the Latin *vocatio,* meaning "a call" or "a summons"). One way to get a handle on ambition is to put the distinction between career and vocation front and center and let it serve as preface and frame to our consideration of the New Testament.

The pastoral vocation is lived out over many years and so, on a mundane level, is experienced as a career much like any other, with its own trajectory, with an inauguration and a conclusion, with highs and lows along the way. The problem comes when career is confused with vocation.

From time to time, students have come to my office wanting to talk about pursuing a PhD in biblical studies, usually in hopes of becoming a seminary professor. I have been around long enough to know that few of them are likely to reach that goal. Even if they have the necessary gifts, there is the expense. Even if they have the funding, there is the fact that not many such jobs exist. Openings are infrequent, requirements are tightly drawn ("Wanted: scholar with expertise in the Gospel of John" = "We already have a Synoptics person."), and competition is fierce. What I say to these inquirers is this: "If you can afford to pay the costs in time and money, if you are motivated by a deep love for the subject and an uncomplicated aspiration to be more useful, then by all means try. But if you are undertaking this with the expectation that it will eventuate in a specific career, you had better think twice." One may exercise a vocation as a scholar and teacher in countless ways. There are only so many ways in which to be a professor with a particular specialization at an accredited seminary of a specific denomination in a certain country.

Pastors who become embittered often get that way due to a misplaced focus on career. That is not to say that ministers should give no thought to where they would be most fruitful, most useful, and most happy. They would be poor stewards of their gifts if they did not. In reality, however, they probably will be required to exercise their vocation in ways and in places they neither expected nor desired. Whether they then flourish has everything to do with their motivation. If the desire of their heart is to be useful, there is limitless need and so endless opportunity. If their sole ambition is to be the pastor of the largest church in the state or the executive director of the denominational mission agency, well, that narrows things a bit.

Again, it is natural to want to employ one's talents to the fullest extent. It is a joy and a privilege to do so, and in a perfect world that would always be possible. This is an imperfect world, however, and only a tiny minority throughout history has had the chance to "be all that they can be." Countless Russian serfs, European peasants, and American slaves might have been able doctors, teachers, engineers, or musicians had the door been open to them. And the situation was that much worse for women of every background and class. These examples may seem extreme, but they are the norm in historical terms.

Most of us are blessed with an array of opportunities, yet each of us still inhabits a specific context that constrains our choices, often in ways in which we ourselves are unaware. Ironically, our choices themselves constrain us. Those who have children assume a vital responsibility that, while fulfilling in itself, limits their ability to fulfill other duties. Every choice in favor of one thing is a choice against countless other things. Every opportunity has costs as well as benefits, though the bright allure of the latter may blind us to the former. In his book *The Contrarian's Guide to Leadership*, Steven B. Sample, former president of the University of Southern California, recalled a conversation with his colleague Vern Newhouse. Said Newhouse, "I've been a careful observer of ambitious men all my life. And here, for what it's worth, is what I've learned: many men want to *be* president, but very few want to *do* president."[4] Sample adds,

> My profession is overflowing with unhappy people who worked assiduously and made enormous sacrifices to become presidents of prestigious universities, simply because they believed that was what they were supposed to do, and in the process gave up their chance to do what it was they really wanted to do and were really good at.[5]

A Successful Failure

A colleague once asked me to teach a session of my choosing in his class on Christian ministry. I decided to tackle a subject I was confident had not been covered, "How to Be a Successful Failure." Most of the students were in their early twenties, and none had gotten as far as graduate school by failing. The world, or at least the church, was their oyster, or so it must have seemed. I attempted to explain that everyone in ministry falls short at times due to their own mistakes, due to the mistakes of others, or due simply to circumstance. A major part of what will eventually define them is how they deal with those failures. They were a polite audience, but my words fell to Earth with a thud. It was a sunny day, and here I was selling raincoats.

---

4. Steven B. Sample, *The Contrarian's Guide to Leadership* (San Francisco: Jossey-Bass, 2003), 160.

5. Sample, *The Contrarian's Guide to Leadership*, 160.

By contrast, mid-career pastors are often relieved and even excited to have the chance to discuss failure. They are experienced, which means they have been beaten up a bit. Their best laid scheme went awry; life rained on their well-planned parade. This is true for pastors with twenty and with twenty-thousand member churches. They have come to understand that being faithful does not always mean being successful, at least not as they had initially defined success.

Of course, I do not mean to say that failure is either good or inevitable. I have no wish to encourage defeatism and resignation. It should be our constant aim to do excellent work to the glory of God. There are few things sadder than watching a dispirited pastor mail it in week after week. No one has been ordained to the vocation of mediocrity. Nevertheless, it is a fact that some soil is more productive and some toil more rewarded. We work the field in which we are placed, adjusting our labors and expectations to its conditions. Success in one patch might look quite different from success in another.

Two examples come to mind from my home state of Illinois. The first is Ulysses S. Grant, who failed at almost everything he put his hand to prior to the American Civil War, but during which he rapidly ascended the ranks, becoming the commander of all Union armies in March 1864. Had there been no great military conflict, it is most unlikely we would have heard of this shopkeeper from Galena. The second example is my own. During seminary, I worked as the youth minister at a small church in Springfield. It was a wonderful place, not least because of the presence of Rev. Bill Zander, one of the finest pastors I have known. Still, the youth group I superintended was tiny. It was a struggle to get six teenagers out on a Sunday evening. After that, I worked at a much larger church up the road in Peoria. Their youth group had experienced some problems, but it soon started to grow and eventually became more than an order of magnitude larger than the one in Springfield. Here I was, the same person doing most of the same things, but with a nearly opposite result. I am grateful to have had both experiences. With only the first, I might have been too hard on myself; with only the second, too easy. In reality, the context was the decisive factor.

They say that cynics are disappointed idealists. I prefer to be an optimistic realist. A realist, because we serve a world that is in many ways broken and dysfunctional; an optimist, because God is with us and will use us despite and even through our failures. In short, what counts is not the impressiveness of our career, which depends to a significant extent upon variables we cannot control, but the performance of our vocation, which is in our hands. At times, the two might be perfectly aligned but at other times diametrically opposed. The good of one's career and the good of one's vocation are not invariably the same.

What has been said about pastors is broadly true for all Christians, although most dentists, mechanics, and hairdressers enjoy a certain occupational freedom unavailable to ministers, especially those under a bishop's appointment. Every believer has a primary vocation as a child of God and as a disciple of Christ.

One's vocation can be lived out in countless occupations. Work is the chief means by which all of us participate in creation. Soon after Robin and I were married, I spent a couple of days building a bookshelf in our new apartment. Like God surveying the cosmos, I at last stepped back, gazed upon my construction, and said, "It is good." Note, I was not comparing my bookshelf to another's shelf: "Yours is good, but mine is better." (That would not have been the likely outcome of such a comparison in any case.) Nor did I think that I had achieved justification by carpentry. Instead, I experienced the joy of being junior partner with the Creator of the universe, of fulfilling my vocation as a child of God in this small way. You might recall the line spoken by the Scottish runner Eric Liddell in the film *Chariots of Fire,* "[God] made me fast. And when I run, I feel His pleasure." To do a worthwhile thing well is part of every Christian's calling, whether pastor or porter, minister or miner.

In his book *The Disciplines of the Christian Life*, written for fellow prisoners during the Japanese occupation of China, this same Eric Liddell wrote that purity "does not mean crushing the instincts but having the instincts as servant and not master of the spirit."[6] That is much the point of this entire book. The same

---

6. Eric H. Liddell, *The Disciplines of the Christian Life* (Nashville: Abingdon, 1985), 72.

could be said of careers: they ought to be our servants and not our masters, vehicles of meaning but not meaningful ends in themselves. For laity just as for clergy, the error is to mistake career for vocation. The former can be lost; the second cannot be taken.

To put the matter another way, a Christian is one who has chosen to live within the vocation of the new covenant (1 Cor 11:25). It is a tradition in British Methodism to hold an annual covenant renewal service to remind believers of this fact. The centerpiece is John Wesley's Covenant Prayer, one of the most moving and challenging pieces of liturgy ever penned:

> I am no longer my own, but thine.
> Put me to what thou wilt, rank me with whom thou wilt.
> Put me to doing, put me to suffering.
> Let me be employed for thee or laid aside for thee,
> exalted for thee or brought low for thee.
> Let me be full, let me be empty.
> Let me have all things, let me have nothing.
> I freely and heartily yield all things to thy pleasure and
>   disposal.
> And now, O glorious and blessed God, Father, Son and Holy
>   Spirit,
> thou art mine, and I am thine.
> So be it.
> And the covenant which I have made on earth,
> let it be ratified in heaven.
> Amen.

To be honest, I wince inwardly every time I pray that prayer, afraid that God might take me up on my offer to suffer, to be laid aside, to be brought low, to be emptied, to have nothing. Nevertheless, this is my vocation as a Christian, to put myself at God's disposal, to live a life that is defined by something, Someone, greater than my career, my possessions, my status. What makes this commitment tolerable is that essential clause "thou art mine, and I am thine." As we have seen so many times before, we are asked to give up one thing only to gain something better.

In sum, we ought to be, are even expected to be, ambitious to fulfill our vocation in Christ. We should want, for example, "to love God with all our heart and soul and mind and strength." One of the major challenges along the way is keeping sharp the distinction between vocation and career. The first is a constant and the second a variable, the first an appropriate end and the second a suitable means. Ambition becomes problematic whenever it inverts that order.

Ambition in So Many Words

What does the New Testament have to say about ambition? Both little and much. Little, because the word "ambition" occurs infrequently (that is, its rough equivalents in the original Greek). Much, in the sense that the New Testament authors were concerned with right motives and energetic action.

The verb that is sometimes translated "to be ambitious" is *philotimeisthai*, a compound of the words "love [of]" and "honor."[7] It occurs in only three places, all in Paul's letters, and each usage is favorable:

> Aspire [be ambitious to] to live quietly, to mind your own affairs, and to work with your hands, as we directed you. (1 Thess 4:11)

> So whether we are at home or away, we make it our aim [our ambition] to please him. (2 Cor 5:9)

> Thus I make it my ambition to proclaim the good news, not where Christ has already been named, so that I do not build on someone else's foundation. (Rom 15:20)

Note the move from the universal to the individual. (The verses

7. Note the discussion of *philotimia* specifically and the role and importance of honor in Greco-Roman society more generally in chapter 5.

are quoted in chronological order, but that does not necessarily mean that Paul's thinking had changed over time.) The command of 1 Thess 4:11 would apply to almost anyone and could just as easily have been written by a Stoic philosopher as a Christian apostle. The second passage is explicitly Christian and concerns the proper ambition of all believers to please Christ. The final verse concerns Paul's own apostolic calling, which is to preach where the Gospel had not already been heard. So, three levels of vocation are evident in these three verses: one human, one Christian, and one specific to the exercise of individual gifts.

At the other end of the spectrum is the word *eritheia*, mentioned in the previous chapter, which is often translated "selfish ambition," "selfishness" or "self-seeking," as in Rom 2:8: "For those who are self-seeking and who obey not the truth but wickedness, there will be wrath and fury" (also Phil 1:17 and 2:3; Jas 3:14, 16). Elsewhere, the word is rendered "dispute" or "strife" (2 Cor 12:20 and Gal 5:20). Taken together, these verses critique a particular sort of ambition in which persons act out of improper self-interest, advancing themselves at the expense of others and causing disharmony and division.

Perhaps the most important word group relevant to the topic is comprised of various forms of the word *zēlos*, "zeal." To be zealous is to "boil over," for example, with fervor and resolve. Today, we associate zeal almost exclusively with religious extremism, especially extremism that compels and justifies terrorism. This is not the case with the New Testament, however, which contains numerous favorable references to zeal, such as the following:

His [Jesus's] disciples remembered that it was written, "Zeal for your house will consume me." (John 2:17, quoting Ps 69:9)

But strive ["be zealous"] for the greater gifts. And I will show you a still more excellent way. (1 Cor 12:31)

[Titus] told us of your longing, your mourning, your zeal for me, so that I rejoiced still more. (2 Cor 7:7b)

[Apollos] had been instructed in the Way of the Lord; and he spoke with burning enthusiasm ["zeal"] and taught accurately the things concerning Jesus (Acts 18:25a)

Now who will harm you if you are eager to do ["zealous for"] what is good? (1 Pet 3:13)

Two references in Paul are especially instructive. The first is in Rom 10:2, in which he says of his non-Christian Jewish contemporaries, "I can testify that they have a zeal for God, but it is not enlightened." Many of Paul's opponents were Jewish, and their "unenlightened" zeal had at times manifested itself as violent opposition. Still, Paul does not say that their zeal is itself the problem. Indeed, "zeal for God" is admirable to Paul, but it can be misinformed and misdirected. The second example concerns Paul's own background:

If anyone else has reason to be confident in the flesh, I have more: circumcised on the eighth day, a member of the people of Israel, of the tribe of Benjamin, a Hebrew born of Hebrews; as to the law, a Pharisee; as to zeal, a persecutor of the church; as to righteousness under the law, blameless. (Phil 3:4b–6)

Paul here is the persecutor, not the persecuted, but the motivating force is again zeal, and once more it is not disparaged. To the contrary, zeal is cited as a positive credential. Paul the zealous rabbi had become Paul the zealous apostle. We might say that he remained thoroughly ambitious, though the object and method of his ambition had changed. Surely, personality plays a role in all of this. Paul would be "Type A" whether he was a Pharisee, an apostle, an athlete, or a stock trader. He was driven, passionate, focused—the sort of person whom we might admire from a distance but not necessarily want to work beside.

The classic statement in favor of such ardor is Rev 3:15–16: "I know your works; you are neither cold nor hot. I wish that you were either cold or hot. So, because you are lukewarm, and neither cold nor hot, I am about to spit you out of my mouth."

Obviously, Paul was not the only one who valued heat, that is, zeal.

The word "zeal" is mentioned negatively about as often as positively, however. In some cases, it is translated with a form of the word "jealousy" or "envy":

> [Stephen said,] "The patriarchs, *jealous* of Joseph, sold him into Egypt; but God was with him." (Acts 7:9)

> Love is patient; love is kind; love is not *envious* or boastful or arrogant. (1 Cor 13:4)

> For where there is *envy* and selfish ambition, there will also be disorder and wickedness of every kind. (Jas 3:16)

Zeal for an inappropriate object is specifically condemned in other verses:

> You covet ["are zealous for"] something and cannot obtain it; so you engage in disputes and conflicts. (Jas 4:2b)

> They make much of you ["they zealously seek you"], but for no good purpose; they want to exclude you, so that you may make much of them ["so that you might zealously seek them"]. (Gal 4:17; the verb *zēloō* is strongly emphasized, appearing as both the first and the last word in the sentence.)

A similar but much less frequently used word is *prothumia*, "eagerness." It is the virtue of the Boreans, who "welcomed the message [of the Gospel] very eagerly" (Acts 17:11). Paul uses the word repeatedly in his discussion of the voluntary collection for the church of Jerusalem: "[F]or I know your eagerness, which is the subject of my boasting about you to the people of Macedonia" (2 Cor 9:2; also 8:11, 12, 19).

Another word group of interest is based on the verb *agōnizesthai*, literally "to agonize," which can be translated "to fight," as in John 18:36 ("If my kingdom were from this world, my followers would be fighting") and in 1 Tim 6:12 ("Fight the good fight"). More often, it is rendered "to strive" or "to contend" and is used positively:

> Strive to enter through the narrow door; for many, I tell you, will try to enter and will not be able. (Luke 13:24)

> [Epaphras] is always wrestling ["striving"] in his prayers on your behalf. (Col 4:12b)

> Athletes ["all who strive"] exercise self-control in all things; they do it to receive a perishable wreath, but we an imperishable one. (1 Cor 9:25)

Episcopal Aspirations

A similar verb with both negative and positive associations is *oregesthai*, meaning "to stretch toward" or, figuratively, "to aspire to" or "long for." Again, the object of the aspiration is what determines whether it is bad or good:

> For the love of money is a root of all kinds of evil, and in their eagerness to be rich [in "stretching toward" it] some have wandered away from the faith and pierced themselves with many pains. (1 Tim 6:10)

> "But as it is, they desire ["stretch toward"] a better country, that is, a heavenly one." (Heb 11:16a)

For our purposes, the most intriguing verse is 1 Tim 3:1:

> The saying is sure: whoever aspires to ["stretches toward"] the office of bishop desires a noble task.

Doubtless, many an aspiring bishop has found aid and comfort in this passage. It is most unusual for a New Testament author to commend self-advancement so straightforwardly. Ideally, the community identifies its own leaders or emissaries in recognition of their gifts and in response to the prompting of the Holy Spirit, as in the story of Acts 13:2: "While they [the believers at Antioch] were worshiping the Lord and fasting, the Holy Spirit said, 'Set apart for me Barnabas and Saul for the work to which I have called them.'" Presumably, neither Barnabas nor Saul spoke this command on behalf of the Spirit.

At least three factors should be weighed in assessing 1 Tim 3:1. The first is that the word translated "bishop," *episkopos*, literally means "overseer," that is, one who looks after or cares for others, much as a shepherd oversees the flock. Beyond that, no one knows what the title actually meant at this time.[8] I once stayed with an Anglican bishop in his lavish official residence. (For the record, he was an excellent bishop, and the stately home that came with the job predated him by several hundred years.) Clearly, that is not the sort of bishopric 1 Timothy had in mind. It might have included oversight of several congregations or only one. There might have been a sole overseer in one location or several.

Second, the fact that the text commends the position as "noble" might be significant. Administrative and pastoral gifts usually come near the bottom of the list (e.g., Rom 12:6–8). Such work was less glamorous than that of being an apostle or prophet. Also, it might have been done at one's own expense. A contemporary analogy is public school teaching. In this country at least, talented college graduates who become teachers do not do so for reasons of money or prestige. The job seldom pays well, and many teachers spend out of pocket to purchase classroom materials. It should go without saying that teaching is undervalued in terms of social status. Consequently, retaining qualified teachers can be as persistent a problem as attracting them. Occasionally, one reads an editorial or hears a radio or television commercial lauding the nobility of the teaching profession, partly to draw new applicants

---

8. A major factor is the dating of 1 Timothy, which is quite controversial. The later the date assigned, the easier it is to imagine the context of a more organized, hierarchical, and professional ministry.

and partly to buck up existing teachers. It is not necessary to tell everyone that a job is desirable if everyone already thinks it is. First Timothy 3:1 might be a sort of PSA (Public Service Announcement) on behalf of the bishopric.

The third factor is the verse's straightforward practicality. We do count on people to put themselves forward for office. I often serve on search committees, and I am grateful for every excellent candidate who submits his or her name. Of course, an outstanding individual might already have been nominated by a third party, but ultimately he or she must agree to being considered. Most searches result in the hiring of only one candidate, which means that perhaps dozens of other worthy applicants were turned down. (Recall the story of Barsabbas in Acts 1:21–26.) That does not make it wrong for them to have offered themselves for consideration. Neither is it the case that search committees always get it right. Lacking the Urim and Thummim (Exod 28:30), both sides are left to formulate their judgments imperfectly.

So, how much "stretching toward" a particular career aspiration is acceptable? Most who would become bishops in my denomination, the United Methodist Church, are required to stretch rather far, that is, to campaign actively for votes. Open and energetic electioneering is of course demanded of those who seek political office, although that was not always the case. (Campaigning for high office used to be done by proxies since advocating for such an honor oneself was thought unseemly.)

I do not have, nor do I expect there is, a simple answer. There are many noble offices to which one might ignobly aspire, and many lowly occupations one might pursue by a high calling. God alone knows the heart. Nevertheless, the many Scriptures we have encountered in this study should guide us as we plot the course of our career and judge our motives. If I had to single out one verse, it would be 2 Cor 5:9: our foremost ambition should be to please God in all that we do. Every other ambition is subservient to that.

This brief word study could be extended, but the results would not change significantly. Ambition of a certain sort is widely commended in the New Testament, just not the sort most of us think of when we hear the word "ambition." Indeed, to be ambitious to please God and to fulfill our calling, our vocation, will frequently require us to choose against conventional ambitions.

A Picture Is Worth a Thousand Words

All of which leads us back to the example of Jesus. Was Jesus ambitious? By conventional standards, not at all. He did not curry favor, did not seek political power, and owned almost nothing. By another measure, however, he was audaciously ambitious, making extraordinary—and to many leading figures, offensive—claims about himself and his messianic vocation. Ambitious to please God? "Your kingdom come. Your will be done, on earth as it is in heaven" (Matt 6:10). "Abba, Father, for you all things are possible; remove this cup from me; yet, not what I want, but what you want" (Mark 14:36).

None of us is Jesus, so what of other, rather more ordinary New Testament exemplars? The post-Easter transformation of Jesus's disciples was in part a conversion of their ambitions. They had become convinced of a new reality within which it now made sense to value what Jesus himself had valued, which allowed them to follow him in ways they could not before. Their ambition and their vocation were no longer at odds, in other words.

Paul had always been ambitious to please God, by his own account excelling beyond his contemporaries in the careful practice of Judaism (Phil 3:4–6). In fundamental ways, however, even Paul's ambition was converted. He came to see the cross as the place where God had acted most directly and decisively in human affairs. It was now the paradigm of his obedience and the shape of his vocation.

Walk through the book of Acts, and you will see the same pattern repeated: the courage of Peter and John, the humility of Barnabas, and the boldness of Stephen. All were both remarkably ambitious and remarkably self-sacrificing. Of course, notable exceptions do exist, including Ananias and Sapphira in Acts 5:1–11, whose dishonest actions were motivated by their desire for money and recognition. Another is Simon, who sought to purchase spiritual power for his own benefit (Acts 8:17–24).

In the previous two chapters, we looked at several of the New Testament epistles, where again we find both positive and negative examples. The act of founding a new church would itself have taken a good deal of what my mother would have called "gumption." So would continuing to care for it from afar, as we witnessed in 1 and 2 Corinthians. Setting aside the issue of who wrote what when, it is noteworthy that each of the apostles associated with the epistles we examined suffered greatly for their faith. According to church tradition, Paul, Peter, and James were martyred, and John was exiled.[9] On the other hand, we have met the "Super Apostles" of 2 Corinthians and the Judaizers of Galatians, and have been repeatedly cautioned against inappropriate ambitions in 1 Peter and 1 John. An additional character in another Johannine letter bears mentioning: Diotrephes of 3 John 9, "who likes to put himself first" and, from the author's perspective, had turned his local church into his own private fiefdom. I would like to know more about Diotrephes. From the author's description, I suspect he was both insecure and ambitious. The two traits do not have to go together, but they often do, and they are a combustible mixture.

I take encouragement from the fact that the New Testament makes plain the early church's uneven record. Paul, Peter, James, and John themselves started badly. The recognition of our own failures can be a hopeful act, an indication that we recognize that our ambitions are also in need of something else, if not initial conversion, then at least fuller sanctification.

The Fire of Ambition

As with other animals, humans possess common drives to varying degrees. Each of us to some extent ambitiously pursues abstract goals, including but not limited to status. We might say that to be ambitious is human, to direct ambition rightly, divine.

---

9. The first three fates are better attested than the last. It was widely believed that John was the only apostle to have died a natural death. Whether this John is the John of the book of Revelation is hotly disputed, however.

The value of ambition in and of itself is therefore ambiguous. It is the fire that warms the house or, unchecked, burns it to the ground. A gifted person who lacks ambition will achieve little. Yes, and the worst people in history have been spectacularly ambitious.

To be or not to be ambitious is thus not the question. Instead, we must ask, "Toward what are we ambitious and why?" The answer may well be elusive. It takes discernment of the sort most likely gained in the company of others who know us well and are permitted to speak to us truthfully. It is also won through searching and open prayer. We might fool ourselves, but we do not fool God.

> O Lord, you have searched me and known me. You know when I sit down and when I rise up; you discern my thoughts from far away. You search out my path and my lying down, and are acquainted with all my ways. Even before a word is on my tongue, O Lord, you know it completely. (Ps 139:1–4)

CHAPTER NINE

Hierarchy

Like so many others who grew up in the 1960s and 70s, I am wary of authority and would prefer to live in a nonhierarchical utopia. Baby boomers and non-boomers alike should be grateful for the social advances of that era, especially in matters of civil rights. Still, an exceedingly fine line divides idealism from naiveté. One of my favorite record albums from the period is Crosby, Stills, Nash & Young's *Four Way Street.* The song "Chicago," written in response to the turbulent 1968 Democratic Convention, climaxes with Graham Nash singing, "Rules and regulations, who needs them? Throw them out the door."

I wonder if Nash's children ever had occasion to quote that line in protest of some unwelcome parental restriction. Sympathetic though I may be toward the loftier ideals of my generation, I have clocked enough time as a parent, a pastor, a teacher, and an administrator to know that a modicum of structure is necessary for any society to function. Throw rules out the front door, and they will find their way in at the back.

I could just as easily have learned the lesson from biology. Animals that live socially have differentiated and often hierarchical roles. That does not mean that all differentiation and hierarchy are good. The fact that they exist in nature does however suggest that they are to some extent necessary. As humans, we have the privilege and the responsibility of consciously determining their degree as well as their shape.

By hierarchy I do not mean class or caste. There is no support for inherited or otherwise arbitrarily assigned position or status in the New Testament, that is, apart from our common inheritance as children of God. What we are considering instead is a fluid and functional hierarchy determined primarily by one's role. Of course, mental constructs allow for tidy divisions. Even in the church, the role that one might play is partly determined by, among other things, the family one is born into. But there is nothing to commend such a system in the pages of the New Testament.[1]

The Art of Biblical Interpretation

Many battles have been waged in the church over issues of authority and hierarchy, often with each side claiming biblical authorization. Consequently, before we investigate how the New Testament might inform our thinking, it is worth pausing to consider the nature of the task.

Appropriating Scripture requires us to work on two distinct levels. The first is the level of the text's original context. Before we apply a passage to our situation today, we need to take care to understand what it might have meant originally. To make this point, I tell my classes a story I heard while participating in competitive rowing, "crew," at Oxford. The university is actually a collection of many separate colleges, several of which have ecclesial names, such as Jesus, Magdalen, St. John's, and my own, Christ Church. Each college could field one or more boats with eight rowers plus a coxswain. The race takes place on the Thames and includes a large bend in the river called The Gut. The stream is too narrow for several boats to race side by side (recall that oxen used to ford here), so they line up along the bank about a boat length and a half apart. A cannon sounds and the race begins. The aim is not

---

1. This is in partial contrast to the Old Testament, in which family lines determine succession in the monarchy and priesthood. Of course, there is ample record within the Old Testament of God raising up leaders without benefit of family connections (e.g., Amos 7:14–15).

to pass but rather to overtake and bump the boat immediately ahead. If that occurs, the two boats exchange places during the next race. Thus it is possible to leapfrog further and further along in the starting order. The boat that crosses the finish line first during the top division's final race is declared Head of the River.

All of which makes perfect sense if you happen to reside in that rarified little world, but it can confound outsiders. The story goes that two American tourists happened to be in Oxford during the Eights Week boat races. One was overheard saying to the other, "I don't get it. I heard someone yelling excitedly that St. John had bumped Jesus in the gut."

You see, it is possible for an interpretation to be literally correct and yet wildly wrong because it ignores the original context. In the present case, we should remind ourselves of the vast political and cultural differences that separate our world from that of the first century, wherein slavery was commonplace, social mobility was comparatively rare, gender roles were rigid, and popular political reform was almost nonexistent. That is the situation within which the first Christians had to organize themselves and make a place within wider society. Much of what they thought was conventional, but some of their thinking did indeed push hard against the received order.

It is also necessary to recall that these were the church's early days, and no one at the time knew that they were constructing an institution that would endure for millennia. Furthermore, their organization was to a significant extent *ad hoc,* varying to some degree from place to place and evolving over the decades during which the New Testament was written. This is why modern churches that seek to replicate the New Testament pattern exactly cannot agree amongst themselves about what it was. It was *not* one thing.

The second interpretive move is that of contemporary application. Given that a text of Scripture says what it said to its original audience,[2] what does it mean for us today? Sometimes

---

2. For the sake of argument, I am greatly oversimplifying the process and limitations of biblical interpretation. Andrew D. Clarke, *A Pauline Theology of*

the application of a text is reasonably straightforward, but often it is not. The classic illustration is passages of the Bible, such as Eph 6:5, that tolerate slavery and command slaves to be obedient to their masters. Had we lived in 1860, this interpretive question would not have appeared abstract. Ought we to accept the norms of first-century society, or do broader biblical principles compel us—who now have the freedom to do so—to change our society into something better, something more in the image of God's reign?

As the world around it changes, the church is pressed continually to make critical and inevitably divisive judgments as to how its Scriptures ought to inform its practices. This is true for all Christians—conservative, liberal, and everyone in between. We fool ourselves if we believe that we simply do what the Bible commands without consideration of modern realities. For example, despite Mark 10:9, the divorce rate amongst evangelical Christians equals or even exceeds that of the general population,[3] and despite 1 Cor 11:5, relatively few churches today insist that all women wear head coverings. The honest and healthy approach is to admit that this interpretive process occurs and to formulate thoughtful and faithful means for engaging in it. The dishonest and unhealthy alternative is to do the interpretive work under the table, pretending that it is not happening. All one has to do is to look at the range of institutional structures adopted by congregations and denominations to see how a church's context has played a role in its appropriation of the New Testament. No apostle was elected to office in the New Testament, but American denominations in particular are, unsurprisingly, fond of elections. Somehow we are convinced this model is superior to the casting of lots, which is

Church Leadership (New York: Bloomsbury T&T Clark, 2012), referenced later in this chapter, contains a helpful section on "Hermeneutical Questions" (18–41).

3. "Fifty Years of Religious Change: 1964–2014," a paper presented by Jerry Z. Park, Joshua Tom and Brita Andercheck at the Council on Contemporary Families Civil Rights Symposium (Feb 4–6, 2014). Available here: https://contemporary families.org/

CCF Civil Rights Online Symposium, February 4–6, 2014

far better attested scripturally (Lev 16:8; Josh 18:6; 1 Chr 24:21; Neh 10:34; Acts 1:26).[4]

The firmest ground is located where high principles are informed by a wide reading of Scripture. That does not mean that we can expect uniformity of outcome, but it ought at least to encourage wisdom and humility, the double helix of virtue. The best of us will get many things right but also some things wrong, especially in the eyes of subsequent generations.

So, given all of these caveats, what can we learn about hierarchy from the New Testament?

The Things That Are Caesar's

The New Testament has little to say about the state or government in general.[5] As far as we know, only a handful of first-century Christians exercised political power (e.g., Sergius Paulus in Acts 13:7). Most believers were from the lower classes. What is more, they hoped for the arrival of the kingdom of God, not the reformation of the empire of Rome. The latter aim would have been unthinkable to the average person in any case. Recall the slave revolt a century earlier that ended with the destruction of Spartacus's army and the public crucifixion of the six thousand captive survivors. The Roman Imperium knew how to send a message.

Christianity inherited from Judaism the belief that human governance operates under God's superintendence (John 19:11; Dan 2:21; Prov 8:15–16; Isa 45:1–3; Wis 6:3), that it is ordained for human good (1 Pet 2:13–14; Let. Arist. 291–92). By no stretch of the imagination does that mean that all governments are beneficent, much less that every act of every government is divinely sanctioned. The Jews themselves had suffered enough under bad

---

4. A New Testament counterexample is Acts 6:3, but it is not clear how the selection of deacons was made.

5. A thoughtful and nuanced overview is provided by Feldmeier, *Power, Service, Humility*, 52–60.

government, their own as well as that of other countries, to know better.

The most famous (or, to some, infamous) statement on the subject in the New Testament comes from Paul's letter to the church in, of all places, Rome. He begins:

> Let every person be subject to the governing authorities; for there is no authority except from God, and those authorities that exist have been instituted by God. Therefore whoever resists authority resists what God has appointed, and those who resist will incur judgment. (Rom 13:1–2)

This is a remarkably optimistic view of civil authority, especially in light of the fact that this selfsame authority later condemned Paul to death. In the account of Acts, however, Roman authorities occasionally came to Paul's aid (e.g., 19:30–31; 22:30; 28:18), and Paul used his Roman citizenship to his advantage (16:38; 22:26), so perhaps the apostle was more sanguine at this point than his later experience would justify.[6]

The underlying issue concerns eschatology, that is, beliefs about the present and future realization of God's plan for creation. Paul made statements earlier in the letter that could be interpreted to mean that Christians already resided in such a superior state of being that they required no external governance and, especially, correction.[7] For example:

> Therefore we have been buried with him by baptism into death, so that, just as Christ was raised from the dead by the glory of the Father, so we too might walk in newness of life. (Rom 6:4)

---

6. The author of Acts made a point of showing that right-thinking public officials, both Jewish and Roman, took a benign if not sympathetic view of the Christians. Even Pilate is said to have known that Jesus was innocent and should have been released (Acts 3:13). The book makes the case that Christianity is not a threat to good order and therefore should be tolerated.

7. "It is possible that Paul's main goal in this passage was to warn Christian enthusiasts who wanted their Christian freedom to spell over into civic life." Moxnes, "Honor, Shame, and the Outside World," 212.

There is therefore now no condemnation for those who are in Christ Jesus. For the law of the Spirit of life in Christ Jesus has set you free from the law of sin and of death. (Rom 8:1–2)

For all who are led by the Spirit of God are children of God. (Rom 8:14)

Paul again demonstrates remarkable theological balance. He states the ideal, but he also knows that his converts were not so fully sanctified as to require no regulation. He goes on:

For rulers are not a terror to good conduct, but to bad. Do you wish to have no fear of the authority? Then do what is good, and you will receive its approval; for it is God's servant for your good. But if you do what is wrong, you should be afraid, for the authority does not bear the sword in vain! It is the servant of God to execute wrath on the wrongdoer. (Rom 13:3–4)

If civil authorities do their jobs under the umbrella of God's authority, then it is necessary to obey them, not simply out of fear, also as a matter of conscience (Rom 13:5–6). Paul concludes: "Pay to all what is due them—taxes to whom taxes are due, revenue to whom revenue is due, respect to whom respect is due, honor to whom honor is due" (Rom 13:7). This is reminiscent of the response Jesus gave to the question, "Is it lawful to pay taxes to the emperor, or not?" (Mark 12:14): "'Give to the emperor the things that are the emperor's, and to God the things that are God's'" (Mark 12:17). Added in Romans is the notion that because they play a necessary role in God's created order, civil authorities are also due respect and even honor.

The framers of the American Constitution were keenly aware that freedom exercised without order would devolve into chaos. They disagreed sharply as to where to strike the balance between individual liberty and general constraint, but it was widely appreciated that monarch and mob could be equally oppressive. Likewise, no New Testament author was as enthusiastic an advocate of individual freedom, at least in the shape of freedom from the law of Moses, as Paul. Yet this same Paul viewed with alarm the bedlam that was the Corinthian church, which necessitated his reminder that "God is a God not of disorder but of peace" (1 Cor 14:33). The Corinthians were told to do "all things" "decently and in order" (1 Cor 14:40) and to submit to proper authority (1 Cor 16:16). The message of Rom 13:1–7 is paralleled in 1 Peter:

> For the Lord's sake accept the authority of every human institution, whether of the emperor as supreme, or of governors, as sent by him to punish those who do wrong and to praise those who do right. For it is God's will that by doing right you should silence the ignorance of the foolish. (1 Pet 2:13–15)

Again, the working assumption is that government is generally benign and its judgments fair. A few verses later, however, the letter takes account of the possibility of injustice: "If you endure when you are beaten for doing wrong, what credit is that? But if you endure when you do right and suffer for it, you have God's approval" (1 Pet 2:20). There is no option to stand up against such unfairness, presumably because such an option did not exist.

It is interesting to compare the view of the state in these texts with the perspective of Rev 13. It is a characteristic of apocalyptic writings to regard the present world order as thoroughly corrupt, even satanic. Rome is therefore portrayed in Revelation as an evil beast that makes "war on the saints" (Rev 13:7). For this author, fiery trial had burned away any conception of the state as divinely sanctioned agent.

Both texts, Rom 13 and Rev 13, are like opposite seats on a teeter-totter, each counterbalancing the other. Together, they correct the tendency to give full weight to half the evidence. Moreover, they show how even in the first century, there was not one Christian perspective on the state. Rather, it varied with circumstance, just as it does for us today.

The Worth of All

Understandably, the New Testament authors were more concerned about matters within the church than without. Insofar as they dealt with issues of structure, their concern was usually the good order (and therefore the good functioning) of Christian communities. Before considering that order, however, we should take note of a crucially important but often overlooked phenomenon: a strong belief in the essential worth of all persons on the part of the New Testament authors.

This perspective should be traced to Jesus himself, who enjoyed the company of the lowly, sought out sinners, made leaders of fishermen, and spoke repeatedly of the reversal of status within God's reign. Jesus did not attempt to win the approval of the rich or the powerful. On the contrary, he honored those whom others overlooked, such as the impoverished woman in the temple:

> A poor widow came and put in two small copper coins, which are worth a penny. Then he called his disciples and said to them, "Truly I tell you, this poor widow has put in more than all those who are contributing to the treasury. For all of them have contributed out of their abundance; but she out of her poverty has put in everything she had, all she had to live on." (Mark 12:42–44)

This is a marvelous story, and it establishes a challenging precedent. Jesus honored not the gift, which was itself modest, but the fullness of the giving. How easily we fixate on the quantity of another's gifts and in so doing fail to notice less prominent yet more faithful stewards. Who are the "poor widows," those doing exemplary but largely unheralded service, in our churches? Whom a Christian community notices says much about the extent to which it already participates in God's reign.

I work at a divinity school that is part of a major university. Given this location, it is understandable that the school participates in the values of the wider academic culture. Given its identity as a Christian school, however, other values, sometimes in tension with those of professional academia, operate. Lining a corridor at Duke Medical School are the portraits of former institutional leaders. Likewise, in one large room at Duke Divinity School hang the likenesses in oils of our former deans. Deans work hard and carry burdens that we faculty do not shoulder, so I do not begrudge them this honor. Still, I found it meaningful when another hallway was lined with the portraits of notable saints, from Augustine to Karl Barth to Billy Graham. Then yet another hallway was populated with pictures, but this time recognizing everyday saints, ordinary Christians with no claim to fame. I have to believe that Jesus was pleased.

Paul reinforced the same outlook, most obviously by insisting that Jewish and Gentile believers were equal partners in the Gospel. We saw in 1 Corinthians that Paul invariably sided with the poor against the wealthy and with the weak against the strong. He argued that all had gifts to exercise and that the church was a body in which all parts were necessary. Authority within the congregation was to some degree charismatic, meaning that it was distributed as spiritual gifts were exercised.[8] Slaves and women were thus enfranchised and could function as leaders. Paul often used familial language, such as "brother" and "sister," which served to undercut previous distinctions, most effectively demonstrated in his support in the letter to Philemon of the slave Onesimus. Finally, like Jesus, Paul believed in the reality of God's coming reign, which relativizes all other claims to sovereignty: "Then comes the end, when he hands over the kingdom to God the Father, after he has destroyed every ruler and every authority and power" (1 Cor 15:24).

The same spirit is evident in, among other places, the book of Acts, which makes a point of saying that the Spirit was given to all

8. On the gradual institutionalization of early Christianity and the process by which specific offices came to be recognized, see Margaret Y. MacDonald, *The Pauline Churches: A Socio-Historical Study of Institutionalization in the Pauline and Deutero-Pauline Writings* (Cambridge: Cambridge University Press, 1988). Chapter 2, "Ministry" (46–60), is of particular relevance to our study. As we shall see, a different perspective is advanced by Clarke, *A Pauline Theology of Church Leadership*.

(2:4, 17; 4:31). The commonality of believers is materially demonstrated in the Jerusalem church's "community of goods," described in Acts 4:32: "Now the whole group of those who believed were of one heart and soul, and no one claimed private ownership of any possessions, but everything they owned was held in common." This arrangement might have been short lived or idealized; nevertheless, this is how the author of Acts wanted to represent the church, that is, as a fellowship in which there was no distinction of wealth. "No distinction" language appears explicitly in reference to the status of Jews and Gentiles. Says Peter in Acts 11:12, "The Spirit told me to go with them and not to make a distinction between them and us," a statement reiterated in 15:9. Similarly, the Gospel is preached "to both small and great" (26:22), and, as in the Pauline epistles, women are gifted and participate alongside men in various forms of ministry (e.g., 1:14; 2:1, 18; 18:26; 21:9).

The common denominator is the belief that God has acted to create a new kind of community, a new kind of people, in which earlier divisions are now irrelevant. The most famous statement to that effect is Paul's in Gal 3:28: "There is no longer Jew or Greek, there is no longer slave or free, there is no longer male and female; for all of you are one in Christ Jesus." This sentiment, though characteristically Pauline, was by no means confined to Paul. According to 1 Pet 2:9–10:

> [Y]ou are a chosen race, a royal priesthood, a holy nation, God's own people, in order that you may proclaim the mighty acts of him who called you out of darkness into his marvelous light. Once you were not a people, but now you are God's people; once you had not received mercy, but now you have received mercy.

The Spirit is the great social leveler. As a rule, Christian groups that place more emphasis upon the present-day empowerment of the Spirit are less hierarchical in structure and provide more opportunities to otherwise marginalized persons. So, for example, it was more common to find women preachers in early Pentecostalism than in contemporary mainline Protestantism. The phenomenon of lay preachers in the Wesleyan movement is a close parallel. Indeed, according to Acts, this is how Gentiles themselves won admission to the church (Acts 10:24–11:18). Said Peter, "If then God gave them the same gift that he gave us when we believed in the Lord Jesus Christ, who was I that I could hinder God?" (11:17). God works through—and sometimes around—existing structures.

Any discussion of hierarchy in the New Testament must take adequate account of texts such as those highlighted above. To focus on offices, such as deacon or elder, without paying due attention to this larger phenomenon is to structure a church that, to paraphrase 2 Tim 3:5, has a form of scriptural authenticity but little power. I am in the business of training ordained ministers, but I am also conscious of the dangers inherent in professionalized ministry. Above all, it may encourage pastors to assume too much responsibility and everyone else too little. Both sides benefit perversely from this arrangement: pastors are all the more essential and parishioners all the less encumbered. No church of the first or twenty-first century fulfills its promise under this arrangement. Indeed, one of the surest signs of a vital church is the active participation of the laity in ministry.

Here as elsewhere, we must be wary of overcorrection. The early church was no egalitarian Shangri-La, a social free for all in which no one exercised authority. The two obvious counterexamples are Jesus and Paul, both of whom characterized themselves as servants and yet both of whom expected followers to obey them— though, it is important to add, not all of their would-be "followers" actually followed. It is hard to imagine any early Christian group in which no one led, however informally. So, it is necessary to keep these ideas in balance or in tension. Christian leadership is inherently paradoxical.

Church Hierarchy

The New Testament unapologetically favors order over chaos, organization over anarchy. Granted, but how much order, and how many layers of organization?

To what extent Jesus himself organized his followers is debatable. He selected the Twelve and gave them a special role as his leading disciples. Within that group, Peter, James and John appear to have formed an inner circle, although it is unclear how deliberate this grouping was or what if any function it performed. In time, Peter emerged as the chief figure amongst all the disciples. He is given formal status as their leader in Matthew's Gospel (16:13–23), a position at least partially confirmed by Paul in Galatians 2:7.

As we have already seen, the list of persons designated "apostles" expanded in the early decades of the church. The two most notable additions to the roster are James, the brother of Jesus, and Paul. Other figures, such as Barnabas and Stephen, emerged as significant figures in their own right within the Jerusalem church.

The founding of semi-autonomous congregations across the Mediterranean basin necessitated local organization and indigenous leadership. There was no universal paradigm, although evidence suggests that leadership was to an extent charismatic, that is, those with recognized gifts were given commensurate authority. For example, according to Acts, the church at Antioch was directed at least in part by a group of acknowledged "prophets and teachers" (Acts 13:1; see also 15:32). The point is made repeatedly that God's gifts were distributed to all, which had the effect (again, to a degree) of decentralizing authority and leveling hierarchy. See, for example, Rom 12:4–8:

> For as in one body we have many members, and not all the members have the same function, so we, who are many, are one body in Christ, and individually we are members one of another. We have gifts that differ according to the grace given to us: prophecy, in proportion to faith; ministry, in ministering; the teacher, in teaching; the exhorter, in exhortation; the giver, in generosity; the leader, in diligence; the compassionate, in cheerfulness.

Nevertheless, not all gifts were equally prized. For example, in 1 Cor 14 Paul ranks prophecy ahead of speaking in tongues because

163

it builds up the whole community and not simply the individual. Two chapters earlier Paul had already written:

> God has appointed in the church first apostles, second prophets, third teachers; then deeds of power, then gifts of healing, forms of assistance, forms of leadership, various kinds of tongues. (1 Cor 12:28)

It is an intriguing list. The first three items are identifiable roles. One may say, "I am an apostle," or, "You are a prophet." After that, things are more nebulous: "deeds of . . . gifts of . . . forms of . . . various kinds of." In addition to the established positions of apostle, prophet, and teacher, Paul affirmed a much wider range of less clearly defined ministries. At the same time, it is hard to escape the fact that apostles are ranked first, presumably because they founded churches and so had a unique role and authority (see 1 Cor 4:15). Likewise, prophets and teachers instructed the communities and so held positions of general responsibility. Moreover, they could function only to the extent that their gift was recognized. One may speak in tongues or render assistance without authority, but it is impossible to teach without others accrediting you as a teacher.

It would be wrong, however, to assert that leadership was based entirely on charismatic giftedness. Most early churches met in private residences,[9] and evidence strongly suggests that the heads of those households exercised leadership over the small groups that met in their homes.[10] So, for example, the married couple Prisca and Aquila are mentioned in Rom 16 along with "the church in their house" (Rom 16:5). The dominant model was thus quite different from what it is today, in which one (potentially quite large) congregation is directed by a member of the ordained

9. See Abraham J. Malherbe, *Social Aspects of Early Christianity*, 2nd ed. (Philadelphia: Fortress, 1983), 60–91 ("House Churches and Their Problems") and Wayne A. Meeks, *The Moral World of the First Christians* (Philadelphia: Westminster, 1986), 108–23.

10. Estimates of the size of these house churches run from ten to forty persons (Clarke, *A Pauline Theology*, 86).

clergy. As John Howard Schütz put it, "Paul does not share the later notion of the Church as composed of clergy and laity, each with unique responsibilities."[11] Instead, there were potentially several lay leaders in a given city, and the whole church of, say, Corinth, would assemble only occasionally.

Studies of church order overwhelmingly focus on three named "offices": overseer (or "bishop"), elder, and deacon. But these terms occur only rarely in the New Testament and then primarily in a few of its later letters. The most popular explanation is to regard the creation of these offices as something that occurred fairly late in the New Testament period. Often, this is contrasted with an earlier and rather idyllic period in which there were no recognized offices and essentially no administrative structure. This reconstruction has been powerfully challenged by Andrew D. Clarke in his recent *A Pauline Theology of Church Leadership*. Clarke points out that even the earliest epistle, 1 Thessalonians, refers to local leaders:

> But we appeal to you, brothers and sisters, to respect those who labor among you, and have charge of you in the Lord and admonish you; esteem them very highly in love because of their work. (1 Thess 5:12–13a)

As does 1 Cor 16:15–16:

> Now, brothers and sisters, you know that members of the household of Stephanas were the first converts in Achaia, and they have devoted themselves to the service of the saints; I urge you to put yourselves at the service of such people, and of everyone who works and toils with them.

The fact that Paul does not mention specific titles does not mean that they did not exist. Moreover, Paul explicitly refers to "overseers and deacons" in Phil 1:1 and calls Phoebe a "deacon of the

---

11. John Howard Schütz, *Paul and the Anatomy of Apostolic Authority* (Louisville: Westminster John Knox, 2007), 7.

church at Cenchreae" in Rom 16:1. (We shall return to Phoebe and the subject of titles below.)

In Clarke's view, "overseers" were primarily heads of households who had responsibility for organizing and teaching the groups that met in their homes. Cities that contained several such groups would have had a council of "elders" made up predominantly, though not exclusively, of such persons. Among other things, this makes sense of the fact that Paul refers to the same group in Acts 20 as "elders" (v. 17) and "overseers" (v. 28). According to Clarke, the work of deacons was "neither menial nor servile, and it concerns the leadership of people, rather than the administration of things." Also, "it may reasonably be deduced that the overseer had greater responsibilities than the deacon, but that there is a measure of overlap in their spheres of duty."[12] The most that can be said is that Clarke's view is plausible. The evidence is too thin to support a weighty conviction, and we must allow for some variance of practice based on local circumstances—points Clarke himself acknowledges. Still, his main contention seems true: early churches had recognized leaders. Scholars have too often idealized and oversimplified this period, perhaps because of their own anti-institutional bias.

Deacons/Ministers/Servants

Of particular interest in the list of 1 Cor 12:28, quoted above, is the word "ministry" (or "service"), *diakonia,* from which comes the English "deacon." The serve/servant/service word group is employed extensively in the Gospels, for example in Matt 20:26, "whosoever will be great among you, let him be your *minister* [or 'servant']," and Mark 10:45, "For even the Son of man came not to *be ministered unto,* but *to minister,* and to give his life a ransom for many." This frequency is unsurprising given that "servant" was one of Jesus's preferred self-designations.[13]

12. Clarke, *A Pauline Theology,* 70.
13. On the many and varied uses of the word group "serve/servant/service,"

Paul refers to both Christ (Rom 15:8) and himself (e.g., 1 Cor 3:5 and 2 Cor 6:4) as "servants," *diakonoi,* along with, among others, Apollos (1 Cor 3:5), Timothy (Phil 1:1), miscellaneous persons (e.g., "us" in 2 Cor 3:6) and even civil authorities (Rom 13:4). Used broadly, "ministry" comprised all of an apostle's activities, including preaching (e.g., Acts 1:17; Rom 11:13; and Eph 3:7). The word is used even more generally with reference to the exercise of spiritual gifts on the part of all believers: "there are varieties of *services,* but the same Lord" (1 Cor 12:5). In Rom 12, however, "ministry" is listed among several distinct roles, so it likely refers to what we would today term "congregational care," possibly including proclamation.

Most debate focuses on the use of the word *diakonos* in Rom 16:1–2:

> I commend to you our sister Phoebe, a *deacon* of the church at Cenchreae, so that you may welcome her in the Lord as is fitting for the saints, and help her in whatever she may require from you, for she has been a benefactor [*prostatis,* a "patron, protector"] of many and of myself as well.

Two key issues engage interpreters. The first, does the word "deacon" in verse 1 refer to a recognized office or to ministry generically? The second, was Phoebe, a woman, here given equal rank by Paul with men who exercised a similar ministry?

The answer to the second question is a straightforward "yes." Paul does not use a feminine form, "deaconess," to distinguish Phoebe's work from that of any other person so identified. Those who want to restrict Phoebe's role must do so on grounds other than this text. Moreover, this is only one of several cases in which Paul uses a single title, including "apostle" in 16:7, for both men

---

see Feldmeier, *Power, Service, Humility,* 51–52. The term does not always refer to a lowly occupation. A servant of the king or of God can enjoy high status, and the word sometimes refers to an authorized go-between or mediator. Nevertheless, the New Testament authors often and characteristically use it to refer to one of menial status and occupation. See the helpful discussion in Clarke, *A Pauline Theology,* 60–71.

and women.[14] Finally, Paul's request that the Corinthians assist Phoebe in her work and his description of her as a "patron" or "protector" indicates that she was a significant figure.

The first question is immeasurably harder to answer. It is part of the larger issue of the early church's organization or "polity," which has been debated intensely for most of the church's history and cannot be covered, much less resolved, here. Why fight over what might seem an arcane or even trivial matter? Because each new grouping within the church has to organize itself, usually over against prior groupings with their own authority structures, all of which sought biblical authorization. Consequently, each New Testament mention of "deacon"—as well as "elder" and "bishop" (which, incidentally, are comparatively rare)—has been both magnified and minimized, stretched and compressed, to fit every conceivable church order.

The matter is complicated even more by the question of the authorship and dating of Acts and the Pastoral Epistles, both of which offer a somewhat different take from that found in Paul's "undisputed" letters.[15] So, acknowledging these difficulties, I shall attempt to present a short overview of the key evidence, acknowledging what cannot be known, which is considerable.

Did Phoebe fill a recognized office? In one important respect, it scarcely matters. However technical or generic the designation, Paul credits Phoebe with doing the work of the Lord and describes her ministry as he does his own and that of other Christian leaders (and, let us not forget, Jesus himself). With the possible exception of Phil 1:1 (see below), Paul elsewhere speaks of being a "minister" in strikingly unspecific terms. On the other hand, mention that Phoebe is deacon of a specific church (at Cenchreae, a seaport to the east) favors this being an actual title, although it still might be

14. For additional examples, review the lists of titles and names near the conclusion of each Pauline epistle.

15. It is interesting to note that Gerhard E. Lenski's view of Paul's supposed social conservatism is based only on a handful of verses in Ephesians, Colossians, 1 Timothy, and Titus. See *Power and Privilege: A Theory of Social Stratification* (New York: McGraw-Hill, 1966), 7. I assert that Paul's perspective has much more in common with that of Jesus than Lenski supposed.

functional in nature. In other words, Phoebe could by virtue of the work she does be widely regarded as a "minister" without actually occupying the appointed office of "deacon."

Those who argue in favor of an early diaconal office cite as evidence Acts 6:1–6, the appointment of seven persons to oversee the Jerusalem church's charitable work. It is unclear, however, to what extent other congregations, especially in the Gentile world, modeled themselves after the Jerusalem church, which was in many ways unique (e.g., James, the brother of the Lord, was its resident leader).[16] Nor do we know if this structure, itself modeled on Jethro's advice to Moses to appoint a group of assistants (Exod 18), persisted.

The church that shows the clearest development in this direction is also the oldest of Paul's European congregations, the church of Philippi. Outside of the Pastoral Epistles, it is only in Philippians that Paul mentions "bishops [*episkopoi*—literally, "overseers" or "superintendents"] and deacons" [*diakonoi*—literally, "servants" or "ministers"]:

> Paul and Timothy, servants [*douloi,* "slaves"] of Christ Jesus, To all the saints in Christ Jesus who are in Philippi, with the bishops and deacons. (Phil 1:1)[17]

Surely, the phrase "bishops and deacons" here refers to specific groups that fulfill certain roles. The fact that the groups are mentioned at all is probably due to the fact that the letter was occasioned by a financial gift received by Paul (4:18), whose collection, presumably, they had supervised. How many such persons there were, what exactly they did, how they came to be so recognized, and how long they served are questions for which we can only wish to have answers.

---

16. There are other problems having to do with the nature of Luke's account in Acts 6-7, but detailing these would add many pages but little certain knowledge to our present study.

17. See the previous chapter for a discussion of the word *episkopos.*

Overseers/Bishops and Elders

We saw in the previous chapter that 1 Tim 3:1–2 refers to the "office of bishop" (NRSV).[18] This is a bit of a mistranslation, however. The original text uses a single word, which we might render in context as follows: "if anyone aspires to oversight, that one is desirous of a good work." There is no "office" mentioned. That oversight is a recognized and commendable function is clear, but we are still a considerable distance from the bishopric as it came to be understood in the second century.

As in the first chapter of Philippians, 1 Tim 3 also mentions deacons (vv. 8–13). Again, their service is commended but not described. It does appear that both deacons and overseers typically arose from within their congregations. There is not yet a professional class of ministers who are accredited and appointed to a locale by an external authority.

The other reference in the Pastorals to overseers/bishops occurs in Tit 1:7–9. This is not joined to a discussion of deacons, however, but "elders" (vv. 5–6; *presbuteroi,* from which, of course, the Presbyterian Church gets its name). It is possible that these were simply two names for the same persons, or it could be that the elders were a larger group out of which some persons were selected for a particular role (that is, as "overseers"), as in Clarke's reconstruction mentioned above.

As if this were not complicated enough, according to Acts 14:23, Paul commissioned "elders" (*presbuteroi*) in the churches he had founded. Given the infrequency of this term in Paul's earlier letters, it seems safest to regard it as a general reference to leaders. The authority of a body of elders was long established in Judaism. The term is used frequently in this way in the Synoptic Gospels and Acts (e.g., Matt 27:41; Mark 7:3; Luke 20:1; and Acts 4:5).

18. We cannot hope to settle questions about the authorship and dating of the Pastorals (1-2 Timothy and Titus). More conservative scholars usually place them near the end of Paul's ministry. Nearly all agree that they represent a later period than Philippians. In any case, they are by no means as definitive with respect to these matters as some claim, so their dating is less significant than might appear.

For its part, 1 Tim 5:17 speaks of elders who "preside over" or "lead" (*proistasthai,* literally, "stand before") the church, only some of whom also preach and teach. Again, this seems to refer to a general body of more experienced or aged persons who oversaw the affairs of the church in a given city. Similarly, James 5:14 and 1 Peter 5:1 also mention church elders, and the author of 2 and 3 John refers to himself simply as "the Elder" (v. 1 in both epistles).

The word we translate "bishop," *episkopos,* shows up in two other places. Acts 20 describes the first part of Paul's final journey to Jerusalem, during which he made a stop at the port city of Miletus on the coast of western Asia Minor. "From Miletus he sent a message to Ephesus, asking the *elders* of the church to meet him" (v. 17). After they assemble, Paul instructs them:

> Keep watch over yourselves and over all the flock, of which the Holy Spirit has made you *overseers* [*episkopoi,* "bishops"], to shepherd the church of God that he obtained with the blood of his own Son. (v. 28)

Here again, oversight of the church in a city was regarded as the function of a *group* of elders. The author of Acts did not have in view the singular office of bishop as it came to be understood by Ignatius of Antioch in the early second century:

> All of you should follow the bishop as Jesus Christ follows the Father; and follow the presbytery [elders] as you would the apostles. Respect the deacons as the commandment of God. Let no one do anything involving the church without the bishop.[19]

The final occurrence is found in 1 Pet 2:25, in which the *episkopos* is Christ himself: "For you were going astray like sheep, but now you have returned to the shepherd and *guardian* ["overseer"] of your souls." Note how the function of oversight is again likened to shepherding. Not incidentally, our word "pastor" comes from

19. Ign. *Smyrn.* 8:1. (Ehrman, *LCL*).

the Latin word for "shepherd." Also, the passage echoes Isa 53, the classic text about the servant of God. So, in 1 Pet 2:25, there is a correspondence between being an overseer and a servant. In other words, Christ acts as bishop, pastor, and deacon.

Ten Lessons

In the second century, circumstances compelled churches to organize themselves more deliberately and in larger clusters. Facts on the ground included the loss of the mother church as a consequence of the destruction of Jerusalem in 70 CE, the death of the founding generation of apostles, the continuing spread of Christianity, the advent of more general political opposition, and the rise of competing and sometimes mutually exclusive versions of the faith. Even without these challenges, some institutionalization was inevitable, but with them, it was imperative.

This period saw the recognition of formal church offices, the most important being that of bishop, who presided over the congregations within a particular area and, ideally, ensured continuity from place to place and generation to generation. Beneath the bishops were the elders. The Latin equivalent of *presbuteros* is *presbyter*, from which we get the English word "priest." Last and too often least come the deacons, whose role has varied considerably over the centuries.

The point is not to argue for one church structure over another. We cannot go back to the first century, nor would any sane person want to do so. The factors that caused churches to shape themselves as they did then do not exist today. If anything, our situation is closer to that of the second-century church. Besides, first-generation Christianity presents us with no uniform pattern to emulate. It does however suggest a number of lessons to which we might wisely attend. Here is my shortlist, to which I hope readers will freely add:

1) Hierarchy, like status and ambition, is ambiguous. It is necessary but not necessarily good, depending on the particulars of the case. The New Testament authors did not reject hierarchy, but

much of what they wrote did serve to undermine the hierarchies of their day. It is interesting to see to which end of this scale later interpreters look for inspiration and confirmation. The fact that both sides of so many controversies—monarchists and revolutionaries, slaveholders and abolitionists, nationalists and internationalists, conservatives and liberals—could find support in the New Testament shows how mistaken is the attempt to replicate the attitude of biblical authors without reference to context, both theirs and ours.

2) All Christians were believed to share in and to be gifted for ministry. Doubtless, this occurred to varying extents and with varying degrees of success, but it is apparent that the idea was taken seriously. Ministry was not the sole responsibility of a paid professional.

3) When distinctions were made between leaders and others within a congregation, the leaders were themselves usually part of a group. Even in today's one church/one (senior) pastor world, it is prudent for leaders to participate in some larger fellowship in which they find both accountability and support. Jesus sent the disciples out two by two for good reason.

4) Form should follow function. In other words, one's role in the church should be determined primarily by one's gifts, not by the office one holds. Even the best pastor is not omnicompetent, though he or she might be under considerable pressure to appear so. There is joy in utilizing our gifts and freedom in admitting what they are not.

5) Charismatic leadership (that is, leadership according to gift) is inherently disorderly, but some disorder is the necessary price of vitality. As they say, nothing is so orderly as a graveyard.

6) Distributing ministry distributes authority. Paul himself found this to be a problem, but he did not therefore renege on his assertion that ministry was shared by all.

7) The tension between charismatic and—albeit, rudimentary—institutionalized authority is found throughout the New Testament and is inherent to the church. At times, that tension manifests itself as conflict. (Think of Peter being forced to defend his going to the home of the Gentile Cornelius in Acts 11.) An entire lack of conflict is therefore either a sign of perfection or else, more likely, gross imbalance or apathy.

8) Structure should not be idealized, but neither should it be repudiated. Somewhere between reverence and refutation lies respect—warranted but not uncritical respect. Considering the dangers on both sides reminds me of yet another 1970s song, The Who's *Won't Get Fooled Again.* An idealistic revolution overthrows the old order, which is replaced by something equally flawed. The song concludes, "Meet the new boss. Same as the old boss."

9) All human structures are impermanent and subject to judgment. That includes states, agencies, and denominations. All leaders are temps.

10) Finally, the church should be the place where the things God honors are honored.

CHAPTER TEN

In Conclusion, Where Do We Start?

So, how do we do it? How do we make the lessons of the New Testament about status and ambition a lived reality and not merely a set of abstract concepts, however interesting and attractive?

I asked myself that question repeatedly as I composed the previous chapters. There is of course no simple, single answer. Moreover, I am reluctant to prescribe for others a fixed or detailed response. The circumstances of readers differ in countless ways, and not all lessons from Scripture are equally relevant—or relevant in the same way—for every believer. In a sense, each reader must write his or her own conclusion, deciding what is valuable and how it applies. Jesus himself rarely explained much less applied his parables, letting hearers sort out for themselves what they meant for them. Happily would I lean on that encouraging precedent, although I suspect my publisher would object!

One thought has dominated my own reflections. It is on that idea that I would like to focus these brief concluding remarks.[1] The previous chapter closed with the sentence "The church should be the place where the things God honors are honored." Let us start there.

---

1. Just prior to submitting my completed manuscript, I discovered Philip Yancey, *Vanishing Grace: What Ever Happened to the Good News?* (Grand Rapids: Zondervan, 2014). Many of the themes touched on in this conclusion are explored in greater detail in Yancey's fine book, which I hope will find a wide audience.

In It Together

The church is often exhorted to live up to its calling as a countercultural community. What exactly it is supposed to counter—materialism, tribalism, nationalism, militarism, racism, sexism, individualism—varies, but the conviction that the church ought to exhibit a distinctive, even radical character is widely advocated. This is as it should be. We need continually to remind ourselves that we are called to a life together that challenges problematic social norms.

Put into practice, few things are more countercultural than the belief that our identity is located in God, not in our worldly status. To state this is easy, but to practice it can be incredibly difficult. By one estimate, the average adult is exposed to five thousand advertising messages per day.[2] We are told incessantly that we could matter, or at least matter more, if only we owned this or looked like that. There is a kind of truth to the claim. Flashy possessions draw attention. (Try showing up for your high school reunion in a Ferrari.) It is consumption, not character, that is envied, and we are pre-programmed to notice physical beauty. (Researchers have demonstrated—to no one's surprise—that a man's cognitive ability declines measurably in the presence of an attractive woman.)[3]

The rewards for climbing the career ladder are palpable, including a higher salary, better working conditions, greater access to power, and increased visibility. Studying in Germany many years ago, I was introduced to the delightful word *titelsüchtig*, meaning "rank obsessed" or "title grubbing." But German professionals are hardly the first or only ones to be conscious of rank. In his *Epigrams*, the Roman poet Martial lamented the loss of revenue he incurred because he had the effrontery to greet his patron, Caecilianus, by

2. J. Walker Smith, Ann Clurman, and Craig Wood, *Coming to Concurrence: Addressable Attitudes and the New Model for Marketing Productivity* (Evanston, IL: Racon Communications, 2005).

3. Johan C. Karremans, Thijs Verwijmeren, Tila M. Pronk, and Meyke Reitsma, "Interacting with Women Can Impair Men's Cognitive Functioning," *Journal of Experimental Social Psychology* 45.4 (2009): 1041–44.

his name and not as "my lord."[4] I work in a modern research university whose business is the conferring of credentials and titles and whose reputation is protected and advanced in ways that Caecilianus himself might envy. The pressure to impress is pervasive and insistent, and we comply in ways both blatant and subtle.

How do we resist? We resist together.

The Christian life is sometimes imagined as a race in which individuals compete (1 Cor 9:24; 2 Tim 4:7). For present purposes, we might better liken it to a team sport. The first apostles founded communities of believers. As we have seen, it was the behavior of their converts *within these communities* that signaled the success or failure of their efforts. Paul enjoined the entire body of Corinthian believers to "be in agreement . . . [with] no divisions among you, but . . . be united in the same mind and purpose" (1 Cor 1:10), and the Philippians to "be of the same mind, having the same love, being in full accord and of one mind" (Phil 2:2). His readers were called to love one another—not an abstraction—by modeling the reign of God within a tangible human connection. They would win or lose together.

Most such congregations met in homes and were quite small by our standards.[5] Everyone could know and interact with everyone else, which must have made things both harder and easier. Harder, because individuals could not hide. These were not like some churches today that one may attend as anonymously as the cinema. Harder, too, because one would be required to deal with persons with whom one might not otherwise associate. Apart from the enigmatic "churches of the Gentiles" (Rom 16:4), early assembles sought to unite disparate groups.[6] Congregations brought different social classes together. Moreover, the cost of participation could be high. In the Greco-Roman world, to align oneself with a group of Christians was to risk alienation from "good society," which was centered on the pagan cult.

4. Martial, *Epigrams* 6.88 (Shackleton Bailey, LCL).

5. Scholars typically estimate the size of the entire Corinthian church at 40-50 members at the time Paul left it.

6. Even churches composed entirely of Gentiles (or Jews, for that matter) likely included persons of different class, educational level, and so on.

Being part of a small Christian community made some things easier.[7] Much easier, in fact. Church is meant to be the place where the reign of God is experienced, not just talked about, where love is demonstrated in living relationships, and where godly character is learned and practiced. In church, the founding stories of the faith are retold and their meaning reinforced. In church, an alternative reality is not only conceptualized; it is demonstrated. That at least is the ideal and the standard against which we ought to judge ourselves.

I do not mean to imply that a church is the only place good things can happen. The world is God's creation, and to the extent that anyone's life is rightly ordered, he or she will experience some measure of the freedom described in this book. Christians are not the only persons who may behave selflessly. Others have set aside worldly notoriety for the sake of some higher good.

Still, such a life should be preeminently possible within the church. Where it is not, where the church simply imposes or mimics the world's status hierarchies, it betrays its Master and belies its message. Recall Jas 2:8–9:

> You do well if you really fulfill the royal law according to the scripture, "You shall love your neighbor as yourself." But if you show partiality, you commit sin and are convicted by the law as transgressors.

The contrast here between love and partiality is noteworthy. We love out of an abundance, and we show partiality out of need. Love gives, and partiality gets. The passage is reminiscent of 1 John 4:18a, *"There is no fear in love, but perfect love casts out fear."*

---

7. On the value of participation in such groups, see Bruce W. Longenecker, "Socio-Economic Profiling of the First Urban Christians," in *After the First Urban Christians: The Social-Scientific Study of Pauline Christianity Twenty-Five Years Later*, ed. Todd D. Still and David G. Horrell (New York: Continuum, 2009), 36–59.

Toward or Away?

According to researcher Evian Gordon, our minds have a simple, binary way of classifying incoming stimuli. Consciously or more often unconsciously, we continuously judge whether the things and persons we encounter are likely to help us or to hurt us. "'Minimize danger, maximize reward' is the organizing principle of the brain."[8] In other words, what we meet is perceived either as a potential reward or a potential threat, creating either a "toward" or an "away" response.[9] It is noteworthy that the brain's limbic (emotional) system reacts far more powerfully to threats than to rewards. As Rock put it, "Human beings walk *toward*, but run *away.*"[10] Moreover, persons experiencing a threat state are less capable of thinking clearly, find it harder to attend to new information, and are more likely to come to erroneous conclusions.

People tend to view others, especially strangers, as possible threats. This disposition was a survival advantage in an earlier age, but it is the source of endless (and mostly needless) problems today. Of course, such behavior is not peculiar to humans. Our cat is a Russian Blue, a breed known to be wary of strangers. She is also a rescue animal that spent time in the wild and is therefore all the more skittish around unfamiliar people and in unfamiliar places. If you visit our house, you will see quite a bit of cat paraphernalia, but you are unlikely to spot the cat, who will be watching you from a safe hiding place.

Many of us are like that cat. Our default state is to be wary and protective not only of our bodies but also of our status. "Just speak-

8. Cited in Rock, *Your Brain at Work*, 105. Cf. Evian Gordon, ed., *Integrative Neuroscience: Bringing Together Biological, Psychological and Clinical Models of the Human Brain* (Amsterdam: Harwood Academic Publishers, 2000).

9. As you would expect, all persons do not respond to potential threats and rewards to the same degree. Studies have demonstrated that relative sensitivity to threats and rewards is at least partly determined biologically and is a major factor in shaping one's personality. See Cain, *Quiet*, and Elaine N. Aron, *The Highly Sensitive Person: How to Thrive When the World Overwhelms You* (New York: Harmony Books, 1998).

10. Rock, *Your Brain at Work*, 107.

ing to someone you perceive to be of a higher status, such as your boss, activates a threat response.... The response can be visceral, including a flood of cortisol to the blood and a rush of resources to the limbic system that inhibit clear thinking."[11] In such a state, one is on guard and thus less creative and less open. It is hard if not impossible simultaneously to defend one's status and to love.

By contrast, to feel loved is to feel accepted, and so to be put at ease and, thereby, to be set free to experience some measure of self-forgetfulness.[12] As with other emotional states, a biological response is at work. When we feel related to others, the brain releases oxytocin, which helps us to be happy and which encourages trust. Indeed, the single factor that most affects human happiness is social relatedness. Christine Carter, a Senior Fellow at the Greater Good Science Center (based at the University of California, Berkeley), notes extensive research on happiness confirms that both the quantity and the quality of one's social connections—friendships, relationships with family members, closeness to neighbors, etc.— are intimately tied to well-being and personal happiness.[13]

Lack of positive relationships is detrimental in similar measure. For example, John T. Cacioppo found "a 30-point difference in blood pressure between those who experienced loneliness and those with healthy social connections."[14]

If we knew the love of God fully, temptations to interpersonal sins such as selfishness, arrogance, rivalry, greed, jealousy, and gossip would hold little allure. It is our perceived need for self-justification that gives energy to so many of our worst tendencies.

---

11. Rock, *Your Brain at Work*, 189.

12. Timothy Keller, *The Freedom of Self-Forgetfulness: The Path to True Christian Joy* (Chorley, UK: 10Publishing, 2014), addresses this subject well. Keller's depiction of the anxious ego as daily "on trial" is an especially helpful image. Brian J. Mahan, *Forgetting Ourselves on Purpose: Vocation and the Ethics of Ambition* (San Francisco: Jossey-Bass, 2002), makes many of the same key points.

13. Christine Carter, *The Sweet Spot: How to Find Your Groove at Home and Work* (New York: Ballantine Books, 2015). Greater Good Science Center: http://greatergood.berkeley.edu/. Cf. Robert D. Putnam, *Bowling Alone: The Collapse and Revival of American Community* (New York: Simon and Schuster, 2001).

14. Rock, *Your Brain at Work*, 163.

I mentioned our cat. Initially, the animal rescue volunteer expressed concern that she (our cat, not the volunteer) was perhaps so edgy as to be unadoptable. It took time, but she gradually warmed to us and now actively seeks our company and attention. She knows she is safe and cared for, so her response is *toward*, not *away*. That the church should provide a *toward* environment almost—almost—goes without saying. Regrettably, many people have experienced it as the quintessential *away* space, a place of judgment, of condescension, of threat. Too often, the ones most drawn to Jesus are the very sort most likely to feel repelled by the church today.

I do not mean to suggest that the church can exist without disagreement and conflict or that it should not challenge both those within and without. But all of that can occur within an atmosphere of mutual regard. Indeed, the church's actions will be more effective if it so pursues them. In a threat state, people close ranks, circle the wagons, batten down the hatches. They are primed *not* to agree or to learn. All of us are willing to accept criticism from a loved one (or even from ourselves) that we would not receive from others.

"Perfect love casts out fear." This is a gift we can give each other. We are the everyday conduits of God's love for the world. We are capable of creating an environment in which the widow's mite is recognized, the marginalized included, and the world's ways of valuing people subverted.

The Religious Question

We have seen that the question of meaning or purpose is at the very heart of human existence. Every one of us in some way is asking, "Do I matter?" And this is the religious question. As William James put it, "Religion in its most abstract expression may be defined as the affirmation that all is *not* vanity."[15] Religion is not cake; it is bread. It is the warp and woof of daily living.

15. William James, *Manuscript Essays and Notes* (Cambridge: Harvard University Press, 1988), 295.

In his brilliant Pulitzer Prize winning book *The Denial of Death,* Ernst Becker characterized human efforts at self-justification, attempts to transcend our true nature as finite creatures, as quests for "heroism." The impossibility of such heroism must be realized for true growth to occur:

> If we put this whole progression in terms of our discussion of the possibilities of heroism, it goes like this: Man breaks through the bounds of merely cultural heroism; he destroys the character lie that had him perform as a hero in the everyday social scheme of things; and by doing so he opens himself up to infinity, to the possibility of cosmic heroism, to the very service of God. His life thereby acquires ultimate value in place of merely social and cultural, historical value. . . . This is the meaning of faith.[16]

Salvation, that commonly mentioned benefit of faith, is the place where there is ultimate meaning, purpose and significance to these lives of ours, despite failure, despite limitations, even despite death. It is both finding and being given that for which we would strive all the days of our lives, the meaning and value of our own existence.

God's acceptance is given freely, graciously. Within such a system there is room for failure, room for the one who comes in second, room even for death. So, we can get off the treadmill; self is no longer on the line, so we can stop worrying about self and be set free to start concerning ourselves with others.

As I read the New Testament, I am struck by the effort its authors expended to create communities within which social barriers could be overcome, social hierarchies transcended, and the socially marginalized accepted. They attempted to manage spaces in which existing social distinctions would not only be overcome; they would become irrelevant, made obsolete by the knowledge of God's perfect love.

It takes effort today, as well. "Being Christian" is a corporate

16. Ernest Becker, *The Denial of Death* (New York: Free Press, 1973), 91.

exercise. We experience God's love—and with it our own salvation, our own justification—*together*. Where that happens, there is the church as the apostles intended it.

BIBLIOGRAPHY

Achor, Shawn. *Before Happiness: 5 Actionable Strategies to Create a Positive Path to Success*. New York: Random House, 2013.

Allen, Pauline, ed. and trans. *John Chrysostom: Homilies on Paul's Letter to the Philippians*. WGRW 16 Atlanta: Society of Biblical Literature, 2013.

Anonymous. *Embracing Obscurity: Becoming Nothing in Light of God's Everything*. Nashville: Broadman & Holman, 2012.

Apostolic Fathers. Translated by Bart D. Ehrman. 2 vols. LCL. Cambridge: Harvard University Press, 2003.

Aron, Elaine N. *The Highly Sensitive Person: How to Thrive When the World Overwhelms You*. New York: Harmony Books, 1998.

Barton, Carlin A. *Roman Honor: The Fire in the Bones*. Berkeley: University of California Press, 2001.

Becker, Ernest. *The Denial of Death*. New York: Free Press, 1973.

Belleville, Linda L. "'Imitate Me, Just as I Imitate Christ': 1–2 Corinthians." Pages 120–42 in *Patterns of Discipleship in the New Testament*. Edited by Richard N. Longenecker. Grand Rapids: Eerdmans, 1996.

Best, Ernest. *Following Jesus: Discipleship in the Gospel of Mark*. Sheffield: JSOT Press, 1981.

Black, C. Clifton. *The Disciples according to Mark: Markan Redaction in Current Debate*. 2nd ed. Grand Rapids: Eerdmans, 2012.

Black, David Alan. *Paul, Apostle of Weakness: Astheneia and Its Cognates in the Pauline Literature*. Rev. ed. Eugene, OR: Pickwick, 2012.

Bowler, Kate. *Blessed: A History of the American Prosperity Gospel*. New York: Oxford University Press, 2013.

Cain, Susan. *Quiet: The Power of Introverts in a World That Can't Stop Talking*. New York: Broadway Books, 2012.

Campbell, William S. *Paul and the Creation of Christian Identity*. New York: T&T Clark, 2008.

Campolo, Anthony, Jr. *The Success Fantasy*. Wheaton, IL: Victor Books, 1980.

Cicero. *Tusculan Disputations*. Translated by J. E. King. LCL. Cambridge: Harvard University Press, 1927.

Clarke, Andrew D. *Serve the Community of the Church: Christians as Leaders and Ministers*. Grand Rapids: Eerdmans, 2000.

———. *Secular and Christian Leadership in Corinth: A Socio-Historical and Exegetical Study of 1 Corinthians 1–6*. Eugene, OR: Wipf & Stock, 2006.

———. *A Pauline Theology of Church Leadership*. New York: T&T Clark, 2012.

Clayton, Philip. "Biology and Purpose: Altruism, Morality, and Human Nature in Evolutionary Perspective." Pages 318–36 in *Evolution and Ethics: Human Morality in Biological and Religious Perspective*. Edited by Philip Clayton and Jeffrey Schloss. Grand Rapids: Eerdmans, 2004.

Deist, Ferdinand E. *The Material Culture of the Bible*. Sheffield: Sheffield Academic Press, 2000.

DeMello, Margo. *Feet and Footwear: A Cultural Encyclopedia*. Santa Barbara, CA: Macmillan, 2009.

deSilva, David A. *The Hope of Glory: Honor Discourse and New Testament Interpretation*. Eugene, OR: Wipf & Stock, 1999.

Dio Chrysostom. *Discourses*. Translated by J. W. Cohoon and H. Lamar Crosby. 5 vols. LCL. Cambridge: Harvard University Press, 1932–51.

Dodd, C. H. *The Parables of the Kingdom*. Glasgow: Collins, 1961.

Feldmeier, Reinhard. *Power, Service, Humility: A New Testament Ethic*. Translated by Brian McNeil. Waco, TX: Baylor University Press, 2014.

Finney, Mark T. *Honour and Conflict in the Ancient World: 1 Corinthians in its Greco-Roman Social Setting*. London: T&T Clark, 2012.

Gladwell, Malcolm. *David and Goliath: Underdogs, Misfits, and the Art of Battling Giants*. New York: Little, Brown and Company, 2013.

Gordon, Evian, ed., *Integrative Neuroscience: Bringing Together Biological, Psychological and Clinical Models of the Human Brain*. Amsterdam: Harwood Academic Publishers, 2000.

Hackman, J. R., and G. R. Oldham. "How Job Characteristics Theory Happened." Pages 151–70 in *The Great Minds in Management: The Process of Theory Development*. Edited by Ken G. Smith and Michael A. Hitt. Oxford: Oxford University Press, 2005.

Harland, Philip A. *Dynamics of Identity in the World of the Early Christians*. London: Continuum, 2009.

Harris, Murray J. *The Second Epistle to the Corinthians: A Commentary on the Greek Text*. NIGTC. Grand Rapids: Eerdmans, 2005.

Harrison, J. R. "Paul and the Roman Ideal of Glory in the Epistle to the Romans." Pages 329–69 in *The Letter to the Romans*. Edited by Udo Schnelle. Leuven: Peeters, 2009.

Heifetz, Ronald A. *Leadership Without Easy Answers*. Cambridge: Harvard University Press, 1994.

Hellerman, Joseph H. *Reconstructing Honor in Roman Philippi*. Cambridge: Cambridge University Press, 2005.

—————. *Embracing Shared Ministry: Power and Status in the Early Church and Why It Matters Today*. Grand Rapids: Kregel, 2013.

Hill, Craig C. *In God's Time: The Bible and the Future*. Grand Rapids: Eerdmans, 2002.

Holmberg, Bengt. "The Methods of Historical Reconstruction in the Scholarly 'Recovery' of Corinthian Christianity." Pages 255–71 in *Christianity at Corinth: The Quest for the Pauline Church*. Edited by Edward Adams and David G. Horrell. Louisville, KY: Westminster John Knox, 2004.

Holmberg, Bengt. *Paul and Power: The Structure of Authority in the Primitive Church as Reflected in the Pauline Epistles*. Philadelphia: Fortress, 1978.

Horace. *Satires. Epistles. The Art of Poetry*. Translated by H. Rushton Fairclough. LCL. Cambridge: Harvard University Press, 1926.

Horrell, David G. *The Social Ethos of the Corinthian Correspondence*. Edinburgh: T&T Clark, 1996.

Howell, Don N., Jr. *Servants of the Servant: A Biblical Theology of Leadership*. Eugene, OR: Wipf & Stock, 2003.

Hurtado, Larry W. "Following Jesus in the Gospel of Mark—and Beyond." Pages 9–29 in *Patterns of Discipleship in the New Testament*. Edited by Richard N. Longenecker. Grand Rapids: Eerdmans, 1996.

Irenaeus. *Against Heresies*. In vol. 1 of *The Ante-Nicene Fathers*. Edited by Alexander Roberts and James Donaldson. Translated by Alexander Roberts. Peabody, MA: Hendrickson, 1994.

James, William. "The Dilemma of Determinism," *Unitarian Review and Religious Magazine* 22.3 (1884): 193–224.

Judge, E. A. "The Conflict of Educational Aims in New Testament Thought." *Journal of Christian Education* 9 (1966): 44–45.

Kaminouchi, Alberto de Mingo. *"But It Is Not So Among You": Echoes of Power in Mark 10:32–45*. New York: T&T Clark, 2003.

Kaplan, Jay R., Stephen B. Manuck, Thomas B. Clarkson, Frances M. Lusso, and David M. Taub. "Social Status, Environment, and Atherosclerosis in Cynomolgus Monkeys." *Arteriosclerosis, Thrombosis, and Vascular Biology* 2 (1982): 359–68.

Karremans, Johan C., Thijs Verwijmeren, Tila M. Pronk, and Meyke Reitsma.

"Interacting with Women Can Impair Men's Cognitive Functioning." *Journal of Experimental Social Psychology* 45.4 (2009): 1041–44.

Keller, Timothy. *The Freedom of Self-Forgetfulness: The Path to True Christian Joy.* Chorley, UK: 10Publishing, 2014.

Kuruvilla, Carol. "Pastor Calls Swanky $1.7 Million Mansion a 'Gift from God.'" *New York Daily News,* October 30, 2013.

Lambrecht, Jan. "Dangerous Boasting: Paul's Self-commendation in 2 Corinthians 10–13." Pages 325–46 in *The Corinthian Correspondence.* Edited by Reimund Bieringer. Leuven: Leuven University Press, 1996.

Lendon, J. E. *Empire of Honour: The Art of Government in the Roman World.* Oxford: Oxford University Press, 1997.

Lenski, Gerhard E. *Power and Privilege: A Theory of Social Stratification.* New York: McGraw-Hill, 1966.

Lewis, C. S. *The Screwtape Letters.* New York: Macmillan, 1962.

Liddell, Eric H. *The Disciplines of the Christian Life.* Nashville: Abingdon, 1985.

Livy. *History of Rome.* Translated by B. O. Foster et al. 14 vols. LCL. Cambridge: Harvard University Press, 1919–59.

Longenecker, Bruce W. "Socio-Economic Profiling of the First Urban Christians." Pages 36–59 in *After the First Urban Christians: The Social-Scientific Study of Pauline Christianity Twenty-Five Years Later.* Edited by Todd D. Still and David G. Horrell. New York: Continuum, 2009.

MacDonald, Margaret Y. *The Pauline Churches: A Socio-historical Study of Institutionalization in the Pauline and Deutero-Pauline Writings.* Cambridge: Cambridge University Press, 1988.

Mahan, Brian J. *Forgetting Ourselves on Purpose: Vocation and the Ethics of Ambition.* San Francisco: Jossey-Bass, 2002.

Malcolm, Matthew R. *Paul and the Rhetoric of Reversal in 1 Corinthians: The Impact of Paul's Gospel on His Macro-Rhetoric.* Cambridge: Cambridge University Press, 2013.

Mandelbaum, Allen, trans. *The Odyssey of Homer.* Berkeley: University of California Press, 1990.

Marcus, Joel. *Mark 1-8: A New Introduction and Commentary.* Anchor Yale Bible 27. New York: Doubleday, 2000.

Martial. *Epigrams.* Translated by D. R. Shackleton Bailey. 3 vols. LCL. Cambridge: Harvard University Press, 1919–24.

Meeks, Wayne A. *The Moral World of the First Christians.* Philadelphia: Westminster, 1986.

———. *The First Urban Christians: The Social World of the Apostle Paul.* 2nd ed. New Haven: Yale University Press, 2003.

Millis, Benjamin W. "The Social and Ethnic Origins of the Colonists in Early

Roman Corinth." Pages 13–35 in *Corinth in Context: Comparative Studies on Religion and Society*. Edited by Steven J. Friesen, Daniel N. Schowalter, and James C. Walters. Leiden: Brill, 2010.

Moxnes, Halvor. "Honor, Shame, and the Outside World." Pages 207–18 in *The Social World of Formative Christianity and Judaism: Essays in Tribute to Howard Clark Kee*. Edited by Jacob Neusner, Peder Borgen, Ernest S. Frerichs, and Richard Horsley. Philadelphia: Fortress, 1988.

Nez, Chester, with Judith Schiess Avila. *Code Talker*. New York: Berkeley Books, 2011.

Nguyen, V. Henry T. *Christian Identity in Corinth*. WUNT 2.243. Tübingen: Mohr Siebeck, 2008.

Park, Jerry Z., Joshua Tom, and Brita Andercheck. "Fifty Years of Religious Change: 1964–2014." Paper presented by Jerry Z. Park at the Council on Contemporary Families Civil Rights Symposium (Feb 4–6, 2014). Available here: https://contemporaryfamilies.org.

Pitt-Rivers, Julian Alfred. *The People of the Sierra*. London: Weidenfeld & Nicolson, 1954.

Pliny. *Letters*. Translated by Betty Radice. 2 vols. LCL. Cambridge: Harvard University Press, 1969.

Plutarch. *Moralia*. Translated by W. C. Helmbold, Harold North Fowler, et al. 16 vols. LCL. Cambridge: Harvard University Press, 1927–2004.

Porphyry. *On Abstinence from Killing Animals*. Translated by Gillian Clark. London: Bloomsbury Academic, 2000.

Putnam, Robert D. *Bowling Alone: The Collapse and Revival of American Community*. New York: Simon and Schuster, 2001.

Quintillian. *The Orator's Education*. Translated by Donald A. Russell. 5 vols. LCL. Cambridge: Harvard University Press,

Rock, David. *Your Brain at Work: Strategies for Overcoming Distraction, Regaining Focus, and Working Smarter All Day Long*. New York: Harper Business, 2009.

Rohrbaugh Richard L. "Honor: Core Value in the Biblical World." Pages 109–25 in *Understanding the Social World of the New Testament*. Edited by Dietmar Neufeld and Richard E. DeMaris. New York: Routledge, 2010.

Roskam, Geert, Maarten De Pourcq, and Luc Van der Stockt, eds. *The Lash of Ambition: Plutarch, Imperial Greek Literature and the Dynamics of Philotimia*. Brussels: Société des Études Classiques, 2012.

Sample, Steven B. *The Contrarian's Guide to Leadership*. San Francisco: Jossey-Bass, 2003.

Sampley, J. Paul. "Paul, His Opponents in 2 Corinthians 10–13, and the Rhetorical Handbooks." Pages 162–77 in *The Social World of Formative Chris-*

tianity and Judaism: Essays in Tribute to Howard Clark Kee. Edited by Jacob Neusner, Peder Borgen, Ernest S. Frerichs, and Richard Horsley. Philadelphia: Fortress, 1988.

Samuels, Amy, and Tara Gifford. "A Quantitative Assessment of Dominance Relations among Bottlenose Dolphins." *Marine Mammal Science* 13.1 (1997): 70–99.

Sapolsky, Robert M. "The Endocrine Stress-Response and Social Status in the Wild Baboon." *Hormones and Behavior* 16.3 (1982): 279–92.

———. "Cortisol Concentrations and the Social Significance of Rank Instability among Wild Baboons." *Psychoneuroendocrinology* 17.6 (1992): 701–9.

———. "Social Status and Health in Humans and Other Animals." *Annual Review of Anthropology* 33 (2004): 393–418.

Šárováa, Radka, Marek Špinkaa, Ilona Stěhulová, Francisco Ceaceroa, Marie Šimečkovác, and Radim Kotrba. "Pay Respect to the Elders: Age, More than Body Mass, Determines Dominance in Female Beef Cattle." *Animal Behaviour* 86.6 (2013): 1315–23.

Savage, Timothy B. *Power through Weakness: Paul's Understanding of the Christian Ministry in 2 Corinthians.* Cambridge: Cambridge University Press, 2004.

Schütz, John Howard. *Paul and the Anatomy of Apostolic Authority.* Louisville, KY: Westminster John Knox, 2007.

Seneca. *Moral Essays.* Translated by John W. Basore. 3 vols. LCL. Cambridge: Harvard University Press, 1928–35.

Shi, Wenhua. *Paul's Message of the Cross as Body Language.* WUNT 2.254. Tübingen: Mohr Siebeck, 2008.

Smith, Huston. *Why Religion Matters: The Fate of the Human Spirit in an Age of Disbelief.* San Francisco: HarperSanFrancisco, 2001.

Smith, J. Walker, Ann Clurman, and Craig Wood. *Coming to Concurrence: Addressable Attitudes and the New Model for Marketing Productivity.* Evanston, IL: Racon Communications, 2005.

Taubes, Gary. *Why We Get Fat: And What to Do About It.* New York: Alfred A. Knopf, 2011.

Thiselton, Anthony C. *The First Epistle to the Corinthians: A Commentary on the Greek Text.* Grand Rapids: Eerdmans, 2000.

Thucydides. *History of the Peloponnesian War.* Translated by C. F. Smith. 5 vols. LCL. Cambridge: Harvard University Press, 1917–23.

Watson, Duane F. "Paul and Boasting." Pages 77–100 in *Paul in the Greco-Roman World: A Handbook.* Edited by J. Paul Sampley. Harrisburg, PA: Trinity, 2003.

Weber, Max. *Economy and Society: An Outline of Interpretive Sociology*. Translated by Ephraim Fischoff. New York: Bedminster, 1968.

Weil, Simone. *Waiting for God*. Translated by E. Craufurd. New York: HarperCollins, 1973.

Witherington, Ben, III. *Conflict and Community at Corinth: A Socio-Rhetorical Commentary on 1 and 2 Corinthians*. Grand Rapids: Eerdmans, 1995.

Yancey, Philip. *Vanishing Grace: What Ever Happened to the Good News?* Grand Rapids: Zondervan, 2014.

Zimmerman, Manfred. "Neurophysiology of Sensory Systems." Pages 31–80 in *Fundamentals of Sensory Physiology*. Edited by Robert F. Schmidt. 3rd rev. ed. New York: Springer, 1986.

SUBJECT INDEX

AUTHOR INDEX

AUTHOR INDEX

James, William, 21n27, 181n15
Judge, E. A., 2n3, 101n35

Kaplan, Jay R., 15n9
Karremans, Johan C., 176n3
Keller, Timothy, 180n12
Kotrba, Radim, 189
Kuruvilla, Carol, 51n20

Lambrecht, Jan, 92n28
Lendon, J. E., 5, 6, 79, 80n11
Lenski, Gerhard E., 168n15
Lewis, C. S., 20–21, 127
Liddell, Eric H., 139
Livy, 81
Longenecker, Bruce W., 178n7
Longenecker, Richard N., 62n3
Lusso, Frances M., 186

MacDonald, Margaret Y., 160n8
Mahan, Brian J., 22n28, 133, 180n12
Malcolm, Matthew R., 48n16
Malherbe, Abraham J., 164n9
Malina, Bruce J., 2n3, 110n6, 111
Manuck, Stephen B., 15n9
Marcus, Joel, 43n5, 72n9
Martial, 176-77
Meeks, Wayne, 2n3, 78, 164n9
Millis, Benjamin W., 78n3, 84n23
Moxnes, Halvor, 79n7, 156n7

Neyrey, Jerome H., 2n3
Nez, Chester, 17
Nguyen, V. Henry T., 96n32

Oldham, G. R., 15n13

Park, Jerry Z., 154n3
Pietersma, Albert, 93n29
Pile, Stephen, 94–95
Pliny the Younger, 50n18
Plutarch, 4n6, 111
Porphyry, 58
Pronk, Tila M., 176n3
Putnam, Robert D., 180n13

Quintilian, 82

Reitsma, Meyke, 176n3
Rock, David, 16, 17n17, 179nn8, 10,
    180nn11, 14
Rohrbaugh, Richard L., 79n7, 81n16
Roskam, Geert, 80n11

Sample, Steven B., 137
Sampley, J. Paul, 99n34
Samuels, Amy, 14n5
Sapolsky, Robert M., 14n7, 15nn10–12
Šárová, Radka, 14n6
Savage, Timothy B., 92n28, 103n38
Schloss, Jeffrey, 10n3
Schütz, John Howard, 165
Seneca, 81
Shi, Wenhua, 17n18
Šimečkovác, Marie, 189
Smith, Huston, 21
Smith, J. Walker, 176n2
Špinka, Marek, 14n6
Stěhulová, Ilona, 189

Taub, David M., 186
Taubes, Gary, 10n1
Thisselton, Anthony, 77
Thucydides, 81n15
Tom, Joshua, 154n3

Van der Stockt, Luc, 80n11
Verwijmeren, Thijs, 176n3

Watson, Duane F., 92n28
Weber, Max, 114
Weil, Simone, 21, 22n28
Witherington III, Ben, 82n20
Wood, Craig, 176n2
Wright, Benjamin G., 93n29

Yancey, Philip, 175n1

Zimmerman, Manfred, 18n20

SCRIPTURE INDEX